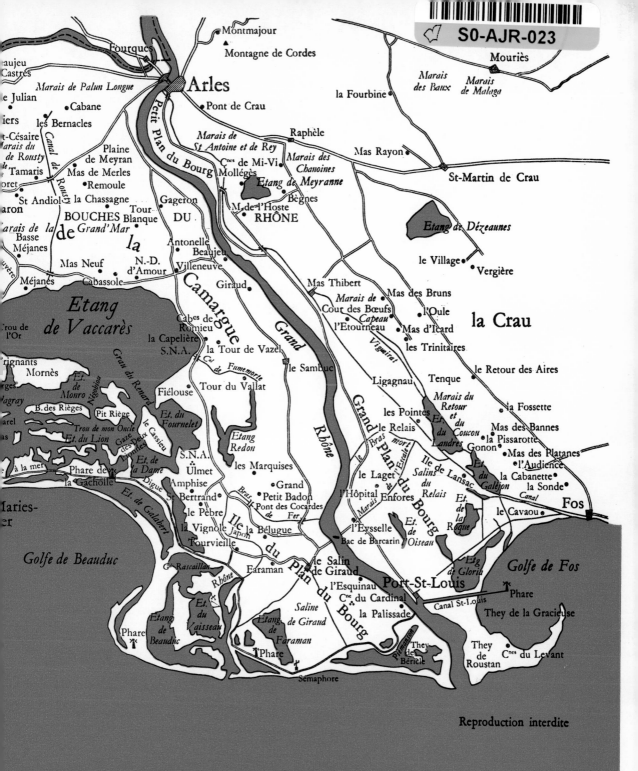

CAMARGUE

CAMARGUE

By MICHEL DROIT

TRANSLATED BY ERNEST AND ADAIR HEIMANN

PHOTOGRAPHS BY

MICHELE BRABO AND SERGE HOLTZ

RAND McNALLY & COMPANY

CHICAGO · NEW YORK · SAN FRANCISCO

Translated from the French

LA CAMARGUE

© B. Arthaud, Paris, 1961

Rand McNally & Company edition published in
the United States and possessions in 1963

Library of Congress Catalog Card Number : 63—15309

Printed in Great Britain

To my father
Thanks to whom I loved the Camargue
Before I knew it
     M.D.

CONTENTS

ILLUSTRATIONS

All illustrations have been gathered together at the end of the
book. Some of these bear captions in French; but a complete list,

MAP

DIAGRAMS
(by Gérard Gadiot)

I

SEASONS OF THE CAMARGUE

THE long track of grey sand, fringed with rustling reeds and tamarisks with a foliage as of green wind, suddenly burst upon me.

As though flattened by a gigantic gust of wind, the immensity of Clamador made all the distance recede sharply, and the horizon dissolve into nothingness.

The earth, black and moist, strewn with purple *salicornia*[1] and blue *saladelles*,[2] slid smoothly down to the transparent water of the Etang des Fourneaux.

Here, three mares galloping like white foam. There, ten black bulls, standing immobile. At my feet, the fresh traces of a herd of wild boar. And over there, a streak on the glistening surface of the marsh, the pink tinge of a line of flamingoes.

This was really the Camargue. Silent and bare, under the opal vault of the sky. Solitary and secret in the complete union of the elements, as on the fifth evening of the creation, when the still virgin world awaited only the coming of man.

And yet the man of the Camargue is there. But all his art and all his talents have, in fact, been devoted to preserving this spontaneous harmony, dating from time immemorial, between sky, earth, water, wind and animals. His presence has never succeeded in reducing the space, in tarnishing the light or in breaking the mystery.

That means that he has known how to protect the three essential qualities of the Camargue.

Even today one's eyes and one's dreams are carried away by the infinite space of the horizons, although this seems to be hewn in proportions fitting both those men who first saw the light of

[1] Glasswort or marsh samphire (trs).
 Statice or sea lavender (trs).

13

day here and their imagination. The ever-changing clarity of air and sky determine the tones of the landscape and compose its harmonies, either drowning its colours or giving them birth. The silence of things unexpressed safeguards its magic.

The search for the Camargue demands above all endless patience and oblivion of oneself and one's habits, for it joyfully dodges roads, motor cars, people in a hurry and those who seek ease and comfort. The rewards of discovering it and grasping it are thereafter given but to few, as is success in love. Many who think that they have achieved it have never been, for it, more than inconstant flirts. Its true lovers are rare, and only a slow and mysterious wooing can lead them to victory. The least infidelity banishes them for ever.

Sometimes, riding alone across the *sansouire*,[3] steeped in grey water, or in the company of a *gardian*[4] friend, helping him to drive along some fifty beasts black of rump and sharp of horn, or again, by moonlight, following the marshy edges of the Lesser Rhone, it seemed to me that I was approaching the goal. . . .

Today, pen in hand, I feel much less presumptuous. Even if it seems to you that you have, in fact, gazed long enough to conquer its space and its luminosity, that you have welcomed its customs and become one with its people, it is not at all certain that the Camargue has, in return, surrendered its soul to you.

Few districts, moreover, are so different according to the seasons, and so acutely sensitive to their passing.

In the spring the waters rise and swell the earth. The salt plants burst into flower. The blue marshlands and the green *roubines*[5] overflow. The *sansouire* seems to float on itself. On the wild islets, in the middle of the lakes to the south of the Etang de Vaccarès, the earth is covered with eggs ready to hatch, for, with noisy, steady flight, the indomitable migrants have returned. The sky is new and pure. The light is as though it were bleached.

Next comes the summer, which dries up everything. Plants and animals live under the continual menace of thirst. Most of the bulls will have reached the pastures of Le Cailar or Canavérier. Those that remain share the scorched grass and the scanty

---

[3] Stretches of alluvial soil, covered with saline plants, which constitute, with the lakes and the marshes, the essential character of the Lower Camargue.

[4] *gardian* : keeper of herds of bulls (trs).

[5] Narrow irrigation canals.

14

shade of the tamarisks or the burnt-up *mourvens*.[6] The earth cracks open, and in places becomes a sort of thick, black jig-saw puzzle, while elsewhere the white, blinding salt crust gleams in the sun.

It is the time of mirages.

But autumn approaches, and with it, deliverance. The sky is overcast with heavy grey clouds, and the first rains soften the brown scales of the soil and soothe its fever.

Storms blast the earth and swell the lakes.

Often a bitter mistral drives the clouds away, and in the golden sunshine of September myriads of blue or red flowers open anew, while the horses' steps quicken and the men's gaze softens.

Winter, however, is not far off, with its misty dawns, its brief days of leaden skies and its twilights of frozen fire.

The *sansouire* is now filled with livid water trapped by the frost. The earth is grey, tawny or violet. Sometimes a haze of snow comes to cover it, and one sees, as though floating there, the transparent ghosts of horses and the heavy, dark shadows of bulls.

For the *gardian* it is a time of great loneliness in the heart of a fantastic universe. It implies an imperceptible rupture with normal concepts of time and space, the oblivion of one's surroundings and long rides with water up to the horse's flanks in search of strayed and threatened animals. They must be moved from one pasture to another, watched over and cared for.

Never is the Camargue wilder, but at the same time more bewitching, than in winter. And, when the evening has come, when the fire of tamarisk or juniper burns in the stone hearth of a hut thatched with reeds, never has the poetry of the delta, crude but tender, lyrical and yet sober, been better expressed than in the singing voices of the men to the flickering of the firelight.

The howling of the wind outside accompanies or dictates the unending flow of words. It unveils infinite paths to the world of secret dreams.

[6] Phoenician juniper.

2

OF SILT AND CENTURIES

THE origin of the Camargue's name has aroused much controversy. Some recognize in it the trace of a far-distant Mediterranean divinity, Camars. Others assert that it is more proper to connect it with Marius, and that Camargue comes from *Caii Marii ager* (the field of Caius Marius). But it is equally possible that the source is to be found in the Celto-Ligurian dialect, where *Ca-mar* signifies 'field covered with water'. Unless, on the contrary, the clue lies in the *langue d'oc*,[1] in which the expressions *cara-marca* (dear frontier) or better still *n'a cap marca* (has no frontier) might conceivably provide the right solution.

On the other hand, the origin of the Camargue's soil does not lend itself to any discussion. One does not even have to be a geologist to identify it. One good look is enough. Pre-eminently an alluvial plain, the Camargue is entirely made up of successive silt deposits left by the Rhone, or rather the Rhones, throughout the ages. The Rhones of Ulmet, Saint-Ferréol, Boismaux and Albaron died slowly, although their memory continues to permeate the countryside. The Greater and Lesser Rhones, however, still embrace it in their ever-changing arms, sallow or wan, tumultuous or almost stagnant, according to the season of the year and the mood of the day.

A geological cross section cut from the earth of the Camargue would enable one to distinguish a top layer, nine to twelve feet in depth, of grey or brown alluvial soil, then a new stratum of black and compact alluvium and finally the same rounded pebbles that one finds in La Crau.[2]

When it has proved possible to drain and then properly irrigate it, the upper stratum becomes fertile soil, as in those regions

[1] One of the old dialects of the south of France (trs).
[2] La Crau is a stony, almost barren plain north east of the Camargue. See map on end papers (trs).

16

planted with vines or cereals which one sees at the apex of the triangle formed by the delta. Lower down and stretching as far as the sea, the land is hidden by water, by plants of the salt marsh and by reeds, which but grudgingly allow the existence of a few scattered islets, either barren or covered with scrub. This is the Camargue of the *gardians*, of the wind and the sun, of herds of animals and of vast horizons whose submerged expanses are dominated by the fortress church of Les Saintes-Maries-de-la-Mer. . . . He who is not fortunate enough to live near the Rhone, from which he can draw fresh water, must therefore concentrate on other things than cultivating the soil.

But the people?

It is probable that the first primitive tribes who inhabited the delta of the Rhone in prehistoric times were attracted to it for reasons of security and, one might almost say, comfort. At that time the branches of the river were numerous, and they cut the existing island of the Camargue into countless islets. These, covered with forests and not denuded as they are today, were therefore relatively easy to defend against possible enemies. Food presented no problems: wild fruit and game abounded on land, and fish in the river. Last but not least, the climate was not generally subject to great variations in temperature.

Nevertheless, with the exception of several carved, or possibly engraved, bones, and two skulls with receding foreheads and accentuated eye sockets, but few vestiges remain of early Camargue man.

Truth to tell, we have in fact hardly any more information than this about the tribes which occupied the Camargue up to the sixth century B.C. Reports that they maintained relations with the Cretans, the Egyptians, the Phoenicians and the Carthaginians, who visited, crossed or skirted the delta, therefore remain confused.

It was after the arrival of the Greeks from Phocaea that the Camargue began to assume sufficient importance to be mentioned in the history of Gaul. Some Ionian merchants, driven out of their country by the Persians six hundred years before the birth of Christ did, at that time, obtain from the Ligurian king of Arles the authority to settle at the mouth of the Rhone and also to found the port which was to become Marseille. When the latter was snatched from them by the Etruscans and the Carthaginians they were none the less able to keep the Camargue and to control navigation on the great river. Remains of foundations, coins, fragments of vases and bits of pottery discovered in the earth of the Camargue bear witness to the passage of Greek civilization on its soil. It is even thought that the first sanctuary to be raised on the present site of Les Saintes-Maries-de-la-Mer was in honour of the goddess Artemis. No doubt this did not prevent divinities of Egyptian origin, such as Isis, Osiris, Râ and, above all, Mithras, from being worshipped there as well.

Later the Gauls drove out the Greeks and invaded Italy before, in their turn, being forced back and conquered by the Romans. The proximity and the prosperity of Arles, which the invaders were about to transform into 'the little Rome of the Gauls', assured a thriving future to the fertile Camargue. Much higher and less marshy than today, irrigated and still wooded, it even became the chosen land of rich settlers and demobilized legionaries, who created towns and villages perched on artificial mounds, cut roads and increased the amount of land under cultivation.

Here again, but little remains excepting vases, bits of pottery and coins. On the one hand, the Camargue, land of sand and water has during the past twenty centuries inundated many man-made buildings. On the other hand, there has always been a lack of stone there, for construction. For this reason, and in defiance of the historical respect due to them, men have not hesitated, when building houses, bridges or roads, to use materials which might perhaps have resisted the engulfment, and might today have served as precious documents to archaeologists for the better writing of history. This is an unfortunate precedent of which the Germans, if they had wished to find excuses, could have availed themselves. As a matter of fact, between 1942 and 1944, they destroyed several country houses, among them Le Simbeu, which had belonged to the Marquis de Baroncelli,[3] to

[3] The Marquis Folco de Baroncelli-Javon, descended from an ancient family of Florentine nobles, *manadier* (owner of horses and bulls), poet, man of deep convictions and candour, is a legendary figure in the Camargue of the *gardians*, for whom he remains '*le marquis*' or (in Provençal dialect) '*lou marques*'. He died in Avignon on December 16, 1943, and his ashes were brought to Les Saintes-Maries on July 27,

construct temporary blockhouses.

When, according to legend, Mary Jacobé, sister of the Virgin Mary, Mary Salomé, mother of the apostles James the Greater and John, their servant Sarah, Lazarus the resurrected, Mary Magdalene and Martha, Maximinius and Sidonius, were set adrift from Palestine on board a boat without sail or oar, they landed on the Camargue coast and found on the present site of Les Saintes-Maries-de-la-Mer a sort of fortress named Oppidum-Râ.

Squeezed between two now non-existent branches of the Rhone, those of Saint-Ferréol and Boismaux, this stronghold confronted at one and the same time the sea and the river, and dominated the navigation towards Arles as well as the exit to the Mediterranean. It was therefore of capital importance. As regards the origin of its name, it is impossible not to see in it the symbol of the sun god of Egypt, father of all the gods. One thing, however, is certain : Râ soon turns into *ratis*, or boat, which may equally have given rise to *radeau*[4] and Rièges.[5] The village that replaced the fortress was, in fact, for long called Notre-Dame-de-Ratis, before being baptized Notre-Dame-de-la-Mer, and only in 1838 Les Saintes-Maries-de-la-Mer.

Very soon the seafarers dispersed to evangelize Provence. Only Mary Jacobé, Mary Salomé and Sarah stayed in the Camargue and founded a first Christian community there. A very old tradition tells of an altar to the Virgin which they are said to have raised with their own hands, probably in the centre of their dwelling, where gatherings of the faithful were held. The excavations ordered in 1448 by King René of Provence, which resulted in finding the remains of the two saints, brought to the light of day, not far from them, a little column and a marble table, considered to be this primitive altar. For, after their death, the saints are said to have been buried in the exact spot where they had lived. According to historians, it is there that the first oratory was constructed, succeeded by a primitive church, and then the

1951. His tomb, raised on the site of his last house, Le Simbeu, has become a place of pilgrimage for all Camargue folk. His daughter Riquette, wife of the rancher Henri Aubanel, zealously keeps alive the veritable cult which local people accord to the memory of the marquis.

[4] In the Camargue, a small island of sand, in the middle of a lake.
[5] The name of a wood described later.

fortress church, which from the eleventh century onwards developed, little by little, into its present form. The spring of fresh water which still rises there is supposed, so runs the legend, to have gushed forth miraculously in the interior of the saints' house, at their command—unless, on the contrary, they chose to live on that spot because of its convenience.

From 465 to 869 Arles suffered no less than ten sieges, and it was taken and pillaged seven times. Visigoths, Franks, Ostrogoths and, finally, Saracens left nothing but ruins, or monuments which were so badly mutilated that even today they give but a very imperfect idea of the splendour of the Roman town. The Camargue and Les Saintes-Maries were not spared, and the work of nature completing that of man, the earth at one time so fertile and dotted with prosperous villages was once more covered with wild forests or alluvial deserts.

The Camargue, nevertheless, was not fated to die, and the memory of its ancient prosperity probably hastened its rebirth. But populating it and cultivating it meant first and foremost protecting it. On the old Roman mounds rose castles such as those of Buzaringue, Méjanes and Albaron. Forts and towers were erected on the islands of the Rhone. Inland, even the country houses were enclosed within ramparts and flanked by look-out posts. Finally, at the mouth of the Rhone, the fortress church which had been built to the glory of the Virgin and the two saints on the site of the latters' sepulchres, became the watch tower and the refuge that controlled and protected the whole countryside. Religious communities settled right across it : for instance Trinitarians at Paty-de-la-Trinité and Cistercians at Ulmet. They rebuilt ruins, constructed villages, cleared, dried out and irrigated the land, planted it and, by their example, encouraged settlers to create houses and hamlets. Little by little, the Camargue took on its true aspect by finding once more some of its ancient wealth and slowly forging its own character.

Geographically speaking, the real Camargue today lies within a triangle 289 square miles in area. Arles is at its apex, and Les Saintes-Maries-de-la-Mer at the mouth of the Lesser Rhone, and Port Saint-Louis at the mouth of the Greater Rhone, are at the two extremities of the base. This essential Camargue is divided up in the following way : 77 square miles of productive land in the north and along the banks of the two Rhones; 139 square miles of *sansouire* and pasture for bulls; 73 square miles of lakes and marshes (of which 34 square miles for the Etang de Vaccarès and over 15 square miles for the smaller lakes).

But the Camargue of the *gardians*, of the horses and the bulls, has long since overflowed these too-restricted limits, as has the silt of the Rhone which gave it birth. It has done this to the west, with the 193 square miles of the Petite Camargue, which ends only at the Etang de Mauguio, not far from Montpellier, and includes the citadel town of Aigues-Mortes, the port of Le Grau-du-Roi and the warmhearted, bull-worshipping towns of Saint-Gilles, Vauvert, Le Cailar, Aimargues and Marsillargues. It also stretches east towards the 77 square miles of the Grand Plan du Bourg and the first flat, pebbly plains of La Crau.

Proud of its origins, faithful to its memories, jealous of its traditions, this Camargue of the *gardians* is for us the true Camargue.

Its kingdom is that of space.

Its religion is that of dreams.

Its god is the bull.

Poised between sky and water, it has known how to remain true to itself, until today it emerges as one of the most unexpected regions in this our twentieth century.

3

THE BULL

I am the bull, roving from Asia
As far as the forests of Liguria,
Where I have reigned
Over the Mediterranean peoples
In joy, in art and in blood.
Marquis de Baroncelli-Javon

ALL along the Provençal valley of the Rhone, and stretching to
Les Saintes-Maries-de-la-Mer, remains of altars used in the cult of
the bull have been discovered. They prove that, in these regions,
the sacrificial slaughter of bulls, appertaining to the religion of
Mithras, was formerly practised. A man, crouching under the
sacred stone, caught the animal's blood on the nape of his neck
and his shoulders in order to draw from it virtue and physical
strength.

Since ancient times, therefore, the bull has inhabited the
Camargue. The Marquis de Baroncelli saw in him the descendant
of the primeval bull, *bos primigenius*, which, after the cataclysm
of the quaternary period, had sought refuge in this estuary of the
Rhone which could 'lull him into the belief that the prehistoric
age was not yet over'. Others consider that he is descended from
the wild ox or the Asiatic, and more specifically, the Persian,
bull. This would explain the simultaneous advent of certain
rituals associated with the cult of Mithras. However that may
be, the bull of the Camargue (*lou biou*), although no longer part
of an ancient ritual, still remains the noblest of animals, the
object of every care and of every passion.

The Camargue is his. He is born there, he lives there and he
dies there, as he has always done. He is such an integral part of
the landscape that it is often difficult to distinguish him from it.

He avoids the proximity of roads, or even that of tracks, preferring the long stretches of *enganos*,[1] the lakes veiled by reeds, or the resin-scented pine woods, wherein to set up his domain, his *querencia*,[2] safe from prying eyes and endless curiosity.

You should catch your first glimpse of the Camargue bull in the early hours of the morning, when his dark form is shrouded in the mist from a marsh. You should see an entire herd move away along the flooded banks of the Lesser Rhone, silhouetted against a red evening sky. You should hear the love combat of the bulls during the night, their raging stampedes, their rapid breathing, their raucous bellowings and their terrifying clashes; finally the triumphant call of the victor, his slow and majestic departure over the still trembling ground and the death rattle of the vanquished. You should catch sight of a solitary beast in the middle of a sweltering summer afternoon, detaching itself from the slim shadow of a juniper bush, and drawing itself up suddenly, facing your horse, an obscure and powerful mass, immobile and sure of itself.

Then, indeed, the bull is truly a sort of god.

In the Camargue, this god has retained its high priests: the *manadiers*.[3]

Baroncelli, Raynaud and Granon will no doubt remain the greatest names of this order of faith and love.

For one does not become rich in the craft of *manadier*, and all the sacrifices, all the struggles and the ungrateful tasks that it entails are only really bearable if one has faith (*la fé*) in the bull and a love of the Camargue, and if one is prepared in advance to accept, as supreme recompense and satisfaction, the barely remunerative glory of owning a fine cocarde bull.

In the Camargue of the *gardians* there are two distinct kinds of stock raising. The first, exclusively devoted to the pure Camargue bull destined for cocarde contests[4] is the one wherein the

---

[1] *engano* is the Provençal name for marsh samphire, the salt marsh plant, which, with the sea lavender, covers the alluvial soil.

[2] In the language of tauromachy, the *querencia* is a place in the ring, usually situated near the barriers, which the bull instinctively chooses as a place of retreat, where he sometimes seeks refuge, and where he may receive the death blow.

[3] A *manadier* is an owner and breeder of herds of bulls and horses (trs).

[4] A cocarde contest is purely one of skill and courage, and the bull is not put to death as in the *mise à mort* or conventional bull fight. See p. 28 (trs).

23

preferences of the big *manadiers* lie. The second is principally orientated towards cross breeding with Spanish blood, with a view to supplying certain local bull fights, for which it would prove too expensive to draw on the cattle breeders of Spain.

The very nature of the soil and its resources, differing greatly according to the seasons, makes stock raising in the Camargue a particularly hard and delicate task. In the summer, when the sun burns up all vegetation and when the salt once more rises to the surface of the earth, it is a matter of finding those places that are the least affected, so that the beasts can graze there. It was for this reason that at one time, from May onwards, the big migrations towards Languedoc and the pastures of Le Cailar took place, when entire herds, surrounded by horsemen, could be seen skirting the sea, crossing the Rhone—sometimes by swimming—and following, by day as well as by night, the tracks leading to the west.

'Towards midnight,' writes André Chamson,[5] 'we would leave the Mas de l'Amarée, driving the bulls before us, shadowy forms in shadow, in front of the shadows of horsemen ranged in a semi-circle. The marquis, riding astride in the centre, would cry out, "It's your turn!" when we had to head back a beast that was straying. At the start the sea of Provence accompanied the tramping of the herd with the sound of its waves, but after a moment it fell silent. We would advance into a gulf of stillness.'

Today, apart from two or three exceptions, the big herds have deserted Le Cailar and remain on the banks of the Rhone or in the meadows of Aigues-Mortes. This makes the summer months even harder for the *manadiers* and their *gardians*.

But with winter returns the perpetual threat of flooding, of frost, of isolated cattle, of long rides in the biting wind, of ice that has to be broken up, of endless counting and recounting, of care to be given and of illnesses to be forestalled. And, until the return of spring, menacing spectres with sharp-pointed horns and sinister black chines ceaselessly haunt the imagination of the *manadiers*, as they recall the seventy cows and bulls belonging to Fernand Granon, blocked by the ice on an island close to

---

[5] A native of the Cevennes, André Chamson belongs heart and soul to the Camargue and is a member of the *Nacioun gardiano* (see p. 36 as well as of the Académie Française.

the Bois des Rièges during the winter of 1929. They died of
hunger, thirst and cold, and it proved impossible to go to their
rescue. Even today, thirty years later, if one scrapes the sand of
the wild islet, beneath the rosemary and juniper bushes, one can
still discover some of the bleached bones of the phantom herd. . .

When it is a year old the bull calf (*vedel*) is called an *anouble*.
It must then be weaned. This is known as the *muselado*. Having
separated it from the cow, and caught and mastered it, the
gardian passes through its nostrils a piece of willow wood,
shaped like a half moon and known as the *museu* or *mourrau*.
Owing to the unaccustomed weight the animal is discouraged
from raising its muzzle towards its mother and instead is
attracted towards the grass and forced to graze.

A little later the branding (*la ferrade*) takes place during the
course of a *gardians'* fête, in the presence of specially invited
members of the public, and the curious. One by one, the riders
pick out from the herd the calves that are to be branded, and
drive them towards the spectators. A *gardian* on foot then has to
seize the young animal, which has usually been thrown by a
blow from a trident,[6] and to immobilize it by holding on to its
horns and by twisting its neck. The owner's branding iron, which
has meanwhile been made red hot over a fire of tamarisk, is then
applied to the left thigh of the future bull. This is known as the
grasiho, a vivid word which describes the sizzling flesh and
charred hair rising from the scar in an acrid smoke. At the same
time a nick (*escoussuro*) is cut in the animal's ear; this follows
the particular *manadier's* motif in the same way as do his branding mark and his device.[7] (The last-mentioned is a cascade of
coloured ribbons fastened to the bulls' withers for the contests.)

From now on the animal can stray at will: whoever finds it
will know immediately to whom it belongs.

When he is two years old, the bull calf is called *doublen*. At
three years he becomes *ternen*. If it can then be seen that he has
the qualities of a great cocarde bull, he is castrated.

In truth, curious as it may seem to the uninitiated, and even
more so to Spanish amateurs of the bull ring, the bull used in

[6] A small, three-pronged iron fork, in the shape of a crescent moon, mounted on
a long wooden handle (see photo no. 19) (trs).
[7] See diagram pp. 70-1.

25

cocarde contests is very rarely a complete male (the celebrated Vovo being the most famous exception) and the stud bulls reserved for breeding are nearly always unaware of the triumphs of the arena. But one should not be misled by that: if the animal, even though castrated, still keeps his name of bull, it is because in his three years of life he has acquired for ever the traits and the temperament of that animal. To keep him integrally male would add nothing to his fighting instincts. Quite on the contrary, he would attain a stage of development which would probably render him practically unsuitable for cocarde contests. In fact, these demand of the bull much speed, power to relax and nervous impulse. Furthermore, a stud bull would also be unnecessarily vicious towards the man in the ring and dangerous to his companions in pasture. During the rutting period, in particular, *manadiers* could sustain heavy losses among their best specimens as a result of the inevitable combats.

The castration (sub-cutaneous lancing) of an almost adult animal is, moreover, not an easy undertaking. He must be segregated and bound, and his kicks must be avoided as he struggles. Often stuffed sacks, in the form of dummies, are stood near the place where the *gardians* operate. As soon as he is freed, the bull charges them, and, after going from one to the other, knocking them over and piercing them, he makes off, in the belief that he has avenged himself on those who have just made him submit to the outrage.

The second world war, the occupation, restrictions and requisitioning were severe blows to the herds of Camargue bulls. By the time of the liberation of France these had disintegrated, as if the animals had been left to themselves for four years, during which frost, epidemics and fights had decimated them without respite.

Today, however, the big herds have regained their vigour. Many others have been created. The cattle of the delta now number close on 4,000 head. And, during the Camargue summer, as at the time of the grape harvest in Languedoc, bull fêtes are more beautiful and more popular than they ever were.

For the *manadier* who has to furnish the bulls for a contest the first task of the day is to pick out the chosen animals. This can prove either rapid or laborious. One day I saw Marcel and

Jean Raynaud, who had set off well before dawn, find within twenty minutes three of the four bulls for which they were looking; but it took them more than an hour to discover the fourth, lying behind a tamarisk by the side of the Lesser Rhone. In the morning mist they had passed and repassed close to him at least ten times without suspecting his presence.

Driven towards the farm, the animals for the cocarde, preceded by a *simbeu* (the leading bull with a bell round his neck) are then directed into the *bouau* (a sort of circular wooden enclosure or corral). From there they go out through a passage hedged in with wood and wicker fencing, called the *embarcador*, before emerging, one by one, into the lorry which is to take them away. For, nowadays, bulls are transported more and more frequently by big motor vehicles, inside which the beasts, fettered by the horns, are wedged tightly one against the other.

All the same, in certain cases, when the pastures are sufficiently near to the bull ring, the selected animals are surrounded by horsemen, who literally fence them in and conduct them thus, first at walking pace and then at a gallop, across fields, tracks, roads and the streets of villages or small towns, as far as the place chosen for the contest.

This, called the *abrivado*, is one of the most spectacular traditional displays of the *gardians* still in existence.

Ten *gardians* are needed to conduct half a dozen bulls in this manner. Three ride in front, so as to curb the animals' speed and to clear a way through the crowd. At each side two more protect the flanks. Finally, three at the back close the circle and, on occasion, hurry on the laggards.

In the sun and the dust raised by the rounded and the cloven hoofs, the approach and the passing of the *abrivado* express all the violence, the heat and the joy of the bull-loving Midi.

The entire population is out of doors, and as soon as the galloping band makes its appearance there are loud cries of: *'Li biou! Li biou! (The bulls! The bulls!)'*

The more audacious spectators advance towards the horses, shouting, gesticulating and sometimes letting off crackers, trying to frighten them and to make them separate, in the hope that a bull will escape. This (*l'escapado*) always provokes general enthusiasm.

27

Only first-class riders, mounted on trained horses, can thus lead an *abrivado* and control the beasts, at the same time preventing and avoiding the traps that are laid in their path.

Nevertheless, when the bulls have at last been safely handed over and penned in the *toril*,[8] the *gardians* slowly retrace their steps and good humouredly look out for those who, five minutes earlier, had tried to make things difficult for them. On the shady pavements outside the cafés, where the *pastis* flows freely, there is now endless chatter. Each one recounts his exploits, real or imaginary, and describes in full detail what would almost certainly have happened if. . . .

The *abrivado* generally takes place about eleven o'clock in the morning, and the contest at three o'clock.

The latter is held either in a real bull ring or in the village, in the middle of a circle of carts placed close together.

The cocarde or rosette is, in reality, a small piece of red cloth, placed in the middle of the bull's frontal bone, and fixed to a piece of string. This stretches from one horn to the other, and is wound several times round them. A tassel of light wool is also attached to the base of each horn.

A first bell marks the entry of the bull into the ring, and a second denotes the beginning of the actual contest. Then the *razéteurs*,[9] dressed in white shirts and trousers, leap in turn towards the animal and, with a hook which each of them holds in his hand, they try to pull off first the rosette, then the tassels and lastly the two bits of string wound round the horns.

The man must obviously calculate to a nicety the direction and speed of his course in order to reach the bull at a given moment and at such an angle that he may strike to the best advantage without being bowled over, gored or trampled upon. After this he will have to break away and, pursued by the animal, rush to the barrier and clear it in his stride, with one leap. Sometimes the bull, carried away by ardour and impetus, follows the man, passing over the obstacle after him, into the circular passage surrounding the arena. Then ensues the bewildered flight of those

[8] An enclosure in the bull ring where the animals are kept before they enter the arena (trs).

[9] Called thus because they pass so close to the bull that they literally graze, or shave, by him.

28

spectators admitted to this part of the bull ring until such time as the animal returns to the field of combat.

For each trophy (rosette, tassel or string) prizes are given corresponding to the difficulties and dangers incurred. If, at the end of the official time, the bull has not been relieved of all his emblems, he is acclaimed by the crowd as the real victor of the joust.

In the Camargue, the great cocarde bulls enjoy a reputation at least equal to that of the most courageous *razéteurs*; this is not unlike the almost mystical respect accorded to the bull in ancient cults.

The long career of Vovo having reached its end, Le Régisseur and some others today attract Provençal lovers of the sport in the same way as does the promise of a Dominguin or an Ordoñez in Spain. But the greatest cocarde bull of all time remains Le Sanglier, from the Granon herd. From 1919 to 1930, he appeared in sixty memorable displays, and the prizes for his strings sometimes reached the astronomical figures of 2,500 to 3,000 francs at that time whilst 500 to 1,000 francs were offered to anyone who touched the animal's forehead, even without removing any trophy, something that has never been seen since. The *razéteur* Rey, whose talent was unequalled, owed his fortune to this bull, and their two parallel careers remain inseparable.

Born in 1916 in the Bois des Rièges, Le Sanglier (The Boar), thus christened by reason of his love of solitude, died of old age in 1933, after having spent his last three years in the courtyard of the farmhouse. All the taurine museums of Provence laid claim to his remains, but these were refused to them. Le Sanglier was, in fact, buried in the rich earth of Le Cailar. A simple monument today marks the site of his last *querencia*, and represents, for all bull lovers of the Camargue and Languedoc, one of the highlights of the taurine tradition.

Few cocarde bulls have had the right to such honours, or anything approaching them. But the funerary lament of an entire herd saluting the death of one of their own kind by making Ramadan, that is to say bellowing in a sinister and heartrending fashion while surrounding his body, is worth a great deal more than all human rites.

Many of the *gardians* assert that they actually saw tears running from the animals' eyes, and that, for a long time afterwards, when certain of them again passed the spot where their companion was buried under the *sansouire*, the lamentations would start up again. In the icy or scorching air, in the whiteness of dawn or the fire of sunset, it then seems as though there passes, over earth and water, the restless and distant protest of an unsatisfied god.

4

GARDIANS AND MANADIERS

Dominating the high Provençal fireplace of the Mas de l'Amarée, the horns of L'Arrogant, one of the proudest cocarde bulls that the Camargue has ever known, pierced the half light.

Twice already, René Barbut, the former *bayle-gardian*[1] of the Marquis de Baroncelli, had filled my glass with a little *rosé*, still rather young, but an honest, fruity wine of his own making. With an old, grey felt hat pushed back, his face dry and burnt, his eyes blue and shining, his two short forearms waving about above the walnut table, he had been speaking for close on an hour in his high-pitched, rolling, thundering and chanting voice —and I did not tire of listening to him.

'In 1925, when I first arrived at the house of the marquis,' he said, 'I was just twenty-three. A wife, two children, my saddle and my *seden*[2]—that was all I possessed. Today, agreed, I may not have a *sou* behind me . . . but I have lived! My brother is station master at Perpignan. That is to tell you that he is not just anybody, and that he earns money! But he has spent his life watching trains coming and going. Whereas I, well . . . I have lived!'

Seated beside her husband, and punctuating each of his words with a nod of her head, Madame Barbut agreed.

'Yes, that's true; we have never had to complain of anything!'

Outside, night continued to fall, and its darkness invaded the dining room of the farmhouse.

'But all that I have and all that I am,' Barbut went on, 'I owe to the marquis. During his life I never did anything except what he told me to do. And even today, when I have to make a deci-

[1] Head *gardian*, a sort of farm bailiff, or manager of a herd.
[2] Camargue lasso, made of plaited and braided horsehair (trs).

31

sion, it is his memory that guides me. . . . Anyhow, the marquis was the greatest expert on bulls that the Camargue has ever known. And that's all there is to it!'

Barbut's face was now lit only by a vague russet glow rising from the well-waxed table, in which the last rays of daylight were reflected. But he went on talking for a long time yet, got up to light a paraffin lamp and open a fresh bottle, and then took up his discourse where he had left off. By the time he had finished he had confined the entire Camargue between the dresser and the glass rack with its thin, carved bars, the taurine trophies fixed to the wall, the fireplace and its mantelpiece bordered with Provençal cretonne and the door of fine mosquito netting which gave out on the night.

The next day, Barbut saddled a horse for me and we went towards the Etang des Launes, to look for the bulls and cows which he wanted to drive towards the Lesser Rhone.

All around us the Camargue stretched into infinity. The animals went at their own pace, and we followed them in silence, for Barbut, so loquacious the night before, this time seemed to be struck by an astonishing dumbness. At times, however, he would let out a raucous cry, strike the flank of his horse with an impatient heel and dash out across a patch of marsh, raising sprays of blue water in his track, in order to catch a straying bullock and lead it back to the bosom of the herd. Then he would return to my side, and we would continue our silent ride, for, when face to face with the Camargue, Barbut knows just as well how to wield the words that express his thoughts as to practise that silence which awakens feeling.

Yes, René Barbut has truly lived the life of his dream, in this land of salt, sand and water, of mirages and mystery. For me he is the incarnation of the true type of pure Camargue *gardian*, of whom fewer and fewer remain: rough and contemplative, wild and trustworthy, simple and poetic. . . .

No one but he has ever spoken to me about the Marquis de Baroncelli with so much true passion and emotion. When the latter, in September 1931, had to resign himself to leaving the Mas de l'Amarée, where he had lived for more than twenty years, but which the owner had just let to the Comte de Montaut-

Manse at a better price, Barbut, his wife and the *gardianou*[3] Battistou were the only ones to help their master with his removal. It was in fact a question of his reaching the new mas, Le Simbeu, an exact replica of L'Amarée, which he had had built in the grounds belonging to the marquise at the mouth of the Lesser Rhone.

Barbut's account of this grim departure was worth hearing.

'At midnight, in driving rain, after the marquis had remained praying for an hour in his empty room on the first floor, we decided all the same to leave. A wagon used for transporting bulls and a small cart contained the furniture of the poor marquis, and we followed, with him, in a forage wagon, his horse, Lou Vibre, closing the ranks. My goodness! How it rained, and what a wind! We were all crying, and it seemed to us that the whole Camargue was weeping to see the marquis obliged to abandon his farmhouse. At dawn, when he had been installed at Le Simbeu, I returned alone to L'Amarée to hand over the keys to Montaut-Manse. I said to him: *"Vaqui li clau dou mas, é lou marques es à l'abri."*[4] The marquis had assured me, "René, you are leaving L'Amarée, but you will return there one day." He foresaw everything. For when Bernard de Montaut-Manse passed on the house to Maître Fontaine, a lawyer of Nîmes who is still my employer, the former called me and said: "Barbut, you gave me the keys of the house. I am returning them to you." I thanked him and asked him to come two or three days later to eat some of Madame Barbut's *bouillabaisse*.[5] "I do not wish to refuse," he said, "but I shall not be able to come." Three days later he was dead, the poor chap!'

When he told me this story, Barbut paused for a moment after he had finished it. How many souvenirs, what regrets, must have been passing through his mind, which his peasant modesty prevented him from voicing! Almost religiously he took the letters written by the marquis out of a cardboard box and let me read them. In every line the greatest noble that the Camargue has ever known expressed his confidence in, and his affection for, the best of his *gardians*.

[3] Apprentice *gardian*.
[4] 'Here are the keys of the house, and the marquis is under cover.'
[5] A fish stew, highly flavoured with saffron (trs).

We had dined that evening in the Barbuts' small house at Les Saintes, its walls studded with photographs and touching mementoes, some of them naïve, with spurs, with *sedens*, with branding irons and muzzles of willow. . . .

Voluble a few minutes earlier, Barbut had suddenly become silent, like the other day, when we had gone to look for the bulls.

'What I am showing you there,' he finally said in a low voice, 'nobody, apart from my wife and myself, has ever seen.'

I knew that he was speaking the truth, and that he was letting me into the secret of his most precious possessions.

'Nobody, positively nobody!'

Madame Barbut nodded assent.

On page after page, in the fine, sloping hand of the marquis, there unrolled before my eyes, couched in the flowery language of a *félibre*,[6] eulogies of faith, generosity, friendship and tender emotion.

'The best of men,' Barbut went on. 'When, in 1951, his ashes were brought from Avignon, where he had died eight years earlier, to be buried at Le Simbeu, the coffin was placed on a hearse surrounded by all the *gardians* on horseback. Well, believe me or not, but the bulls understood what was happening. On each side of the embankment they accompanied our procession, and many of them bellowed as though it were Ramadan. We had never seen the like of it, and we shall never see it again in the Camargue.'

I was not of an age, nor had I had the luck, to know the Marquis Folco de Baroncelli-Javon.

That evening, however, I truly believed that I had sensed his mysterious presence.

In reality, there is a little of Baroncelli in all true Camargue *manadiers*, and in every genuine *gardian*.

Faith, passion, an uncompromising fidelity to the country and its traditions and a freshness of spirit. . . .

They are his heirs and, in one way or another, they continue his work.

To think of the *manadier* as a simple stockbreeder, and the

---

[6] Member of a society of Provençal poets and scholars, founded by Frédéric Mistral (trs).

gardian as a commonplace cowherd would, moreover, be a serious mistake. Their craft, in truth, contains a particle of priesthood, and the way in which they practise this, a breath of poetry, which the marquis knew how to raise to the highest degree.

The *manadier* and the *gardian* seem to be sons of the sky, the earth and the water, those three essential and intermingled elements of the Camargue. They sense its mysteries in the same way as they respect them. They instinctively perceive its language, its silence and its symbols.

This sort of religion among the *gardians* is, moreover, frequently secular, for the founding of the brotherhood of *gardians* (the Confrérie des gardians de Bouvine et de Rossatine de Camargue), one of the oldest in France, dates back to January 2, 1512.

A notary of Arles, Maître Jouve, conserves their original archives and statutes, and every year, on the Sunday in April nearest to Saint George's Day, the ancient brotherhood celebrates the fête of their patron saint.

On each occasion this is a memorable day for the old Roman city.

In the morning, along the Boulevard des Lices, the *gardians* assemble on their white horses. Their trousers are either of dark moleskin, or 'devil's skin' (small black-and-white checked material), tight at the knee, widening out at the ankle and decorated down the side with black piping; a brightly coloured shirt, either spotted or flowered; and a short jacket of black, braided velvet. Their faces, tanned with the salt air and burnt by the sun, are shaded by wide-brimmed felt hats. In his right hand each one proudly holds a trident, resting on his stirrup, whilst from that of the captain flutters the blood-red and gold standard of the brotherhood, on which is embroidered a picture of Saint George overcoming the dragon. This has been brought from one of the museums in the town, where it remains all the year round.

From all the narrow streets emerge groups of Arlésiennes, wearing with grace and dignity their shawls, their lace bonnets and their dark skirts in voluminous folds. Presently the men appear, with their drums and fifes. After this a colourful, musical procession is formed, whose first stop is the church of Notre-Dame-de-la-Major, near the Roman arena, where a grand solemn mass is celebrated, accompanied by Provençal hymns. Then the horsemen and their mounts receive a blessing in the square in front of the church. After that the procession marches slowly through the town, with a salute to the mayor, the sub-prefect and the notary who keeps the venerable archives. In the immense, sunny courtyard of the school of the nuns of Saint-Vincent-de-Paul, the *gardians* and the men and women of Arles religiously intone the *Coupo Santo*, the anthem of the people of the Midi.

Finally, after a lively banquet, everybody meets at the arena, where Provençal contests alternate with equestrian displays by the *gardians*.

But the rules which have existed for more than five centuries in the heart of the brotherhood are not limited to arranging the rites of the annual festivities. They provide, especially among the *gardians* of the Camargue, a solidarity which has never been called in question and a fidelity to all the regional traditions, of which there are, in France, few equivalent examples.

Let us add that, in 1904, the Marquis de Baroncelli founded the *Nacioun gardiano*, a company of horsemen and Provençal poets. This in no way rivals the brotherhood, but is perhaps more attentive to everyday folklore, and is also more literary, though equally devoted to the protection of Camargue traditions.

Its first captain was Jousé d'Arbaud, the author of *La Bête du Vaccarès*. The poet Alphonse Arnaud succeeded him.

This fidelity to himself summarizes the man of the Camargue.

Without it there would be no more *manadiers*, no more *gardians*, no more bulls and no more horses.

That is why, even if it is difficult to establish a hierarchy among so many men burning with the same faith, for me the Raynauds remain the typical *manadiers*. It is in them that the traditions of the *gardians* spring from the most profound depths and always flow on uninterruptedly.

For eighty-five years the Raynauds, from father to son, have in fact been devoted to the rearing of bulls.

At the head of the line is Mathieu Raynaud, apprentice *gardian* at the age of eleven, then *gardian* and later the head *gardian* to

Gustave Papinaud, one of the originators of modern breeding methods.

Then, when Papinaud died in 1903, in accordance with his last wishes his entire herd, if not strong in numbers at least rich in the quality of the strain, became the property of Mathieu Raynaud.

The latter, called 'Papé Raynaud', is still one of the greatest names associated with the rearing of the Camargue bull, and the cross breeding that he undertook, before 1914, between his bulls and the cows of the Baroncelli herd, has remained celebrated from Le Cailar to Les Saintes-Maries.

When he retired, soon after the war, Mathieu Raynaud was succeeded by his son Joseph who, twenty-five years later, in turn handed the herd on to his two sons Casimir, the elder, and Jacques.

Meanwhile, the Raynaud *manade*[7] had progressed in all fields and had supplied the contests with a good number of unforgettable cocarde bulls, such as Catalan, Greffat, Bajan, Valdemore, Hérisson, Marinero and so on.

But, as we have seen, the second world war and the occupation proved to be relentless towards the breeding of Camargue bulls. A difficult and ungrateful task thus confronted Casimir and Jacques Raynaud. Nevertheless, once again the future of the family was assured, for Casimir had two sons, Marcel and Jean, who could not imagine life in any other way than under the purple and red colours of the *manade*.

This knowledge certainly helped to ease the last moments of Casimir Raynaud, who died, prematurely, of a heart attack in 1959. He knew that the line would continue.

Today, Jacques Raynaud and his two nephews reign over a good 300 animals, which are to be found, according to the season, at Canavérier, near Aigues-Mortes, or as far away as Le Grand Radeau, Le Ferradou and Le Sauvage, bordering on the Lesser Rhone. And there is hardly a big cocarde display in the Camargue or in Languedoc at which the Raynaud herd is not represented.

It will continue thus for a long time.

A knowledge of breeding almost uninterrupted and passed on

[7] A collective noun incorporating bulls, horses and the complete set up (trs).

by word of mouth, an unfailing attachment to the country, to its past and its rites, a strong sense of the responsibilities imposed by the name they bear, and an absolute respect to the head of the family make the Raynauds truly the most authentic *manadiers* in the Camargue.

5

THE HORSE

IT is on horseback that you should ramble across the Camargue.

From the height at which you are seated you can look at the country from the best angle, and your mount, whether walking or galloping, knows instinctively the exact pace suited to exploration.

It is generally considered that the Camargue horse is of North African origin and that it was established in the delta by the Carthaginians, the Moors or the Saracens. Later on, it is said, Julius Caesar, impressed both by its stamina and its vivacity, decided on and encouraged its breeding, and even went so far as to create stud farms. Then the horse of the Camargue is believed to have reverted to its original state, its taste for freedom and its wild life.

Others, however, believe that it comes from Asia, like the bull, but this time from Tibet or Chinese-Turkestan.

Only one thing is certain: in the same way as the bull, the Camargue horse has lived long enough between the branches of the Rhone to have become a pure product of the district. The sun, the wind, the salt marsh plants and the waters of the river have made him what he appears today. And when you see him galloping bare and free along the sea coast, his form, his coat and his movements harmonize so well with the waves breaking on the pale sand that you would say he was born of the foam of this Mediterranean which no doubt holds the key to the mystery of his origins.

Grey at birth but very soon turning white, and small of stature, the horse of the Camargue rarely exceeds fourteen and a quarter hands at the withers. His silhouette is robust and thick set, and his joints are strong. His hoofs are of so hard a horny matter that he can easily do without horseshoes. His neck is muscular, his brow wide and flat, his eyes very deep set, his muzzle rounded and his nostrils wide open. But it is his long mane and his tail that sweeps the ground that give him at one and the same time his character and his nobility.

The horse of the Camargue is naturally lively and strong. He dislikes trotting, and can hardly be said to shine at it, but will pass most willingly from a slightly ambling gait—tiring to the uninitiated—to a rapid, very supple gallop which is remarkably successful in avoiding the thousand and one obstacles in his path. Exceptionally abstemious, he is generally not used to oats, the salt in the grasses and the vegetation of the marshes being sufficient to ensure his outstanding endurance. He is not scared of doing thirty miles a day, and people in the Camargue like to recall that the Marquis de Baroncelli, mounted on Sultan, and accompanied by Jacques Marignan, the then mayor of Les Saintes, rode from Les Saintes-Maries-de-la-Mer to Lyon and back, that is about 280 miles, in forty-three hours.

But the greatest and most precious quality of the Camargue horse is his extraordinary knowledge of the bulls. Born near them, in the same wild surroundings, having grown up beside them and led the same free life, having eaten of the same plants and quenched his thirst, like them, with the water from the canals or the Rhone, he knows remarkably well how to 'stick' to the animals, anticipate their swerves, swing round with them, avoid their charges and cut off their retreat. He has an instinct for sorting them out, and no scientific cross breeding would be able to replace the pure Camargue horse for working with the bulls.

The Camargue *gardians'* manner of riding, like that of everyone for whom the horse is above all a means of transport and a professional tool, would hardly satisfy discriminating purists. But at least it exactly suits the animal, as it does the country.

The *gardian's* saddle consists of a cantle in the form of a back rest—like that of a cowboy or a Mexican herdsman—and a very high pommel flanked by two saddle bags. The stirrup is a sort of metal cage which beginners are wise to mistrust if they do not wish to have one foot trapped when they fall.

Well seated on the saddle, his chest slightly in, his legs almost stretched at full length and his heels outward, the *gardian* becomes one with his mount in the most efficient way. Even if he is not a classical rider he is audacious to a rare degree, and absolutely sure of himself on horseback, because riding has always been natural to him as an essential element in his life. Indeed, it comes so naturally to him that he rides just as easily bareback as with a saddle. Round the animal's muzzle the *gardian* knots the *mourraioun*, that is to say a lasso which serves as a bridle and of which he holds the end; then, jumping on the horse's bare back, he becomes hardly distinguishable from his mount. Their bodies merge into one shape, as though they had always been predestined for each other, and, like a centaur, they gallop past behind the white-coated mares, seemingly born of the same soil, and modelled and nourished by the same wind, as the herd that they are pursuing. . . .

The breaking in of a Camargue horse is however difficult, for its wild character and love of liberty render it averse to carrying a saddle and even more to submitting to the wishes of man.

First of all the animal that you wish to train must be separated from the herd and led into the corral, the fenced enclosure which, as we have seen, is also used for marshalling the cocarde bulls before they are transported.

The second operation consists in catching the horse with a lasso, and then mastering it. This is not without danger to the *gardians* for, as soon as the horse feels the harsh contact of the rope on his shoulders, and then the brutal pressure of the slip knot, he almost goes mad. He kicks, rears, leaps and tries to escape; he turns over on his back, beating the air with all four legs and lashing out blows with his hoofs, the whole punctuated by terrible whinnyings.

The *gardians* must on no account let go, and at the end of the struggle they have to pass the halter round the horse's nose. This enables them to lead him, exhausted but not vanquished, to the stable where he will remain, more or less hobbled, for about ten days, so that he will gradually get used to the presence of men. They will come to look at him, and later pat him affectionately but carefully. When the time comes they will begin by throwing a blanket over his back. Later, as soon as they sense that he is in a better mood, they try to make him carry a saddle without

41

stirrups. They will take him out into the corral and make him walk up and down and turn with the help of a leading rein. At last, when he seems to accept the weight of this first burden, he is properly saddled and girthed. Then one of the men mounts on his back and tries to remain there in spite of the way that he leaps, kicks and shies. This is the *débrandage*, the *gardians'* private version of the rodeo, in which their greatest risk is that of being trapped beneath the horse. For, in order to rid himself of his unwelcome guest, the animal often finds nothing more effective than suddenly to turn over sideways and vigorously roll on his back.

The man does not always win the first round of this struggle, nor even the second. Nevertheless, if he has held on all through a session, he is generally accepted, or at least tolerated. But it still implies long and patient hours of work in the corral, and many jaunts, before the horse becomes a really reliable mount, that is to say, ready to carry a rider other than his first master, to respond to heels and reins, to accept putting his instinctive knowledge of the country to the service of the one whom he is carrying and to submit to the work expected of him.

A Camargue horse, moreover, never breaks entirely with his heredity and his profound instincts, and after several years of good and loyal service he may still seize an opportunity of proving to his master of the moment that he has remained first and foremost a son of the wind, of chance and of liberty. Then again, more than one dashing classical horseman—and recently one of the best known in France—has been seen to mock at the stocky outline and somnolent air of the sorry steed which was going to throw him without hesitation a few seconds later.

There is, properly speaking, no large-scale rearing of horses in the Camargue. As a rule they are used only in connection with guarding the bulls, and they are therefore bred solely as required for this work. At least this was so up till the last few years, for the increase of excursions on horseback for tourists—to which we shall return later—has created new needs.

That is why, today, more and more Arab horses are being imported. But, if they are perfect for the beginner, their feeble stamina, their fear of water and, above all, their lack of natural ease when in contact with the bulls make them on the contrary but mediocre mounts for the *gardians*. All the same, crosses of Arab and Camargue strains do sometimes give good results. This does not prevent the majority of *manadiers* and *gardians* from remaining faithful to the pure product of the district, at least in so far as their favourite mounts are concerned. And one would never see a rider of the *Nacioun gardiano* take part in a folklore festival or a procession mounted on a horse whose genealogical tree had not had its roots planted in the moist and salty soil of the delta since time immemorial.

A love of the Camargue implies, in fact, an equal attachment to the black silhouette of the bull and the white profile of the Camargue horse.

Thus the memory of Lou Vibre, the favourite mount of the Marquis de Baroncelli, is inseparable from that of his master in the minds of all. Young folk in the Camargue learn the horse's name in the same breath as that of their most celebrated man.

Lou Vibre was buried standing up, an honour reserved to this day only to the great horses of the Camargue.

How many times will not a lonely *gardian* have seen three white, bare, forms galloping away by moonlight across the *sansouire* or the livid marshes! And will he not have taken them for the ghosts of Le Prince, Lou Vibre and Sultan, or of others whose memory haunts his faithful and sentimental soul?

6

JUNIPER AND FLAMINGOES

A FINE, grey rain, whipped by the west wind, drowned the earth, the sky, the Etang de Malagroy and even the silhouette of François, the *gardian* from Cacharel, who, ten yards ahead of me, slowly advanced with the water rising up to his stirrups.

We found our feet once more on a sandy islet whose stunted vegetation resembled dried moss, and our two horses relaxed a little after their watery passage by galloping along a pale, sandy shore. Then we crossed a new arm of the lake and landed on the first island of the Bois des Rièges.

Botanically speaking, the Bois des Rièges is, without doubt, the richest, the most fascinating and the best preserved part of the Camargue. Moreover, a special permit is required if one wishes to go there, and this wise precaution fortunately safeguards its solitude and its wildness of spirit.

The wood, in fact, consists of a broken chain of seven islets, separated by *gazes*[1] and covered by low thickets as dense as the African bush.

The Phoenician juniper (*mourven*) predominates. Generally it is a small tree, with a rough, twisted trunk and dark green foliage slightly resembling that of the cypress. The soil of the Camargue is the only one in France to which it has adapted itself. Of exceptional resistance, it can survive there for several centuries, and the fact that the famous bull Le Sanglier was born in the shade of a juniper of Rièges has made these trees for ever dear to the hearts of Camargue folk.

As soon as we reached the edge of the wood our horses knew instinctively how to trace their way across the narrow natural paths, how to find the gentlest slopes both to climb and redescend the brushwood-covered dunes and how to avoid the thorny gar-

[1] Stretches of not very deep water.

44

lands of sarsaparilla. In other words, they soon showed themselves to be the most gifted of botanical guides.

The sweet scent of wild rosemary mingled with the pungent and clinging perfume of the juniper, whose dark, narrow, rough foliage contrasted with the more supple and smoother leaves of the wild olives. From time to time we crossed a small clearing where a fresh-water pool made a blue stain in the middle of the marsh samphire. Then, after having found a passable track between two thickets of lentisc trees, we once more penetrated the wood.

To speak of the monotony of the flora of the Camargue would be to make a grave mistake or to give way to the sort of deceptive illusion to which the hasty visitor is often prone.

Quite on the contrary, everything may change according to the region and the nature of the soil, sometimes even from one strip of land to another separated from it only by a lake.

To the north, or along the *segonnaux*[2] of the Rhone, one finds the fertile zones of the agricultural Camargue, where vines, asparagus, lucerne and, nowadays, rice are grown.

As for the Camargue of the *gardians*, which is the one that interests us, we have seen that it starts lower down, descends as far as the sea, and even spills over on the east and the west beyond the branches of the Rhone.

First and foremost, it consists of the waste lands or *sansouire*, the long stretches of alluvial soil with saline vegetation. Here the marsh samphire (known locally as *engano*) reigns supreme, growing in rounded tufts, grouped together or spaced out. These plants, with their hard stems and lumpy tips, green in spring, grey in summer and reddish in winter, cover the soil and impart their colours to it.

Beside the marsh samphire grows the sea lavender, whose fragility is only apparent, and whose tiny blue or purple flower is the *gardians'* emblem.

---

[2] Long, narrow tracts of land between the actual banks of the branches of the river and the embankments which have been raised on either side of them to prevent flooding (trs).

This flower so pretty
Which covers thy space in millions
For thee, O Camargue, is the crown
That destiny sent you from on high.

Charles Naudot

Apart from the marsh samphire and the sea lavender, quite a diversity of other plants which are not always noticeable at a first glance grow on the alluvial soil. Sea rushes with long, tufted stems, wild iris, sea purslane, water mint and so on.

In the marshes, in plumed reed beds, grow various species of reeds, whose flexible stalks wave like long hair or manes in the wind.

In spring and summer a green moss floats on the lakes; the water carries it towards the little sandbanks, where it dries and turns brown, still retaining the imprint of the tide that brought it there.

Lastly, on the sand dunes, grow the tamarisks of delicate silhouette, whose tender foliage merges with the wind, the blue thistle with metallic, wounding leaves, the Mathiole lily with its heavy perfume, the tiny wild marguerite and the sea rocket, whose scrubby tufts are covered with strange, lilac-coloured flowers. . . .

Of the one-time immense forests there remain but few traces, apart from the Bois des Rièges and the pine woods of Clamador and Brasinvert in the Petite Camargue. On the other hand, a number of farm houses, particularly near Aigues-Mortes, still enjoy the spreading shade of a group of parasol pines.

But to classify the flora of the Camargue is a very difficult task, because its character is so changeable, depending as it does on the type of soil, natural irrigation or favourable winds.

One day Marcel Raynaud gave me rapid proof of this. We had left the pine trees of Brasinvert, with their dark branches and scent of resin, crossed La Grande Rhée Longue, the extreme point of the Etang du Cabri, on horseback, and struck at once across the lands of Le Grand Radeau. There there were grass, rushes and tufted juniper bushes, giving their protective shade to the bulls. Then we crossed the waters of the Etang d'Icard, with their floating mosses, and arrived at Le Sauvage. This time a flat, bare plain, which could have been painted by Yves Brayer,[3] stretched out before our eyes. Here was the traditional *sansouire*, barely carpeted with marsh samphire and sea lavender, where the black bulls stood out against the tawny background. We stopped at last at that loop of the Rhone known as Le Reculat. On the far bank tamarisks were growing, amid whose green, misty foliage white horses were mirrored in the calm water of the river.

We had not done two and a half miles, but the Camargue's flora and appearance had changed five times before our very eyes.

As far as the fauna of the Camargue is concerned, quite apart from the bulls and the horses, and considering the limited space, it is one of the richest and most varied stretches of country in Europe.

In the Camargue, first and foremost, the bird is king. To realize this it is not even necessary to visit, in the company of a keeper, the admirable reserve instituted by the Société Nationale d'Acclimatation de France (the French National Society of Acclimatization) on the borders of the Etang de Vaccarès. It is sufficient to traverse the countryside and keep one's eyes open.

I remember one day in May accompanying a fisherman of Les Saintes to the first islets of the Etang dit l'Impérial. We had started out in the small hours from the Pointe de Jonquas. The flat, narrow boat slid across the still grey water. As far as the horizon, thousands upon thousands of pairs of wings made the sky twinkle with white stars—and, strange phenomenon, the noise of the wind and the cries of the birds surrounded us and yet did not succeed in breaking the silence of the lake. There was the whistling of the avocets, whose beaks are the shape of a shoemaker's curved awl, the squealing of the Mediterranean gulls, and the two-note cry of the herring gulls which, apparently influenced by the spirit of the countryside, shouted in their raucous voices: '*Toro. . . toro. . . .*'

The sun rose slowly.

[3] Yves Brayer, the designer of the jacket of this book, has devoted a great part of his work to the Camargue. Moreover, he lives for several months each year in the Cabanes de Gines, quite close to Les Saintes-Maries.

The sky turned blue.

Over there, where sky and water met, the silhouette of Les Saintes-Maries-de-la-Mer resembled the mysterious, pale capital of a distant Atlantis, already half engulfed.

First of all we set foot on the island of Redouière. Alarmed by our approach, its inhabitants had evidently taken flight in a cloud of trembling wings, but they had had to leave behind their most precious treasures, which they would find again after our departure : the eggs of the spring clutches.

As far as the eye could see the earth was carpeted by them. The mustard-coloured, speckled eggs of the avocets, whose nests consist of a few twigs gathered together on the damp sand; then those of the herring gulls, which lay their eggs on dried water moss that they have placed between tufts of marsh samphire. There were many other types of eggs, in particular those of wild ducks, but these last were so perfectly hidden in the hollows of clumps of rushes that it was only when a mother less timid or more foolish then the rest flew off in front of us as we passed near to her that we were able to discover her hiding place.

In short, we had to move forward with infinite care, and never has the expression 'treading on delicate ground' seemed more apt, for we had to pick our way with great precision to avoid crushing or even touching with our feet the many eggs scattered in our path.

Even outside the reserve the Camargue is one of the greatest nesting places in Europe, in the same class as Lake Balaton, the Danube delta or Andalusia. Many resident birds of France and also numerous migrants—approximately 150,000 a year—meet there; they like the solitude, the peace and the security that they enjoy in the Camargue, and they call there on their autumn and springtime journeys.

Web-footed birds, marsh birds and waders of course predominate. The first include innumerable mallards and other types of duck. The second consist mainly of moorhens and coots. Among the third are snipe and sandpipers, the black-and-white avocets, little egrets with their fine, white plumes, purple herons, bitterns booming lugubriously in the fog of the marshes, the glossy ibis—a rare and precious guest—and last of all the irreplaceable pink flamingoes.

In all the Camargue these last have the most delicate and harmonious plumage. Whenever they stretch their moving pink line, in bands of a thousand or fifteen hundred, across one of the grey lakes, the temptation to approach within three hundred yards of them is one of the most irresistible and hopeless of the many that this region has to offer. The flamingoes are nevertheless there, quite near, delicate, willowy forms, standing on two slender legs, their beaks, in the form of a *cesta*,[4] groping about in the mud.

But the lookout has a sharp eye, and if the rider discreetly advances ten yards the flamingoes, with great dignity, retire the same distance.

The game continues for as long as the flamingoes judge that they have a sufficient margin of safety.

If the man cheats and passes beyond the permitted limits, with a call more peremptory than the rest the pale pink line glides slowly on to the surface of the water, rises, and changes into a floating, hazy cloud of pink silk, framed by the fiery red and black lines of the feathers at the wing tips. Then the cloud spreads out again, turns, passes overhead and finally disappears like the misty streaks of the setting sun, drowned in an azure lake. . . .

Of the whole of France, the flamingoes know only the Camargue, whose moist and transparent immensity may perhaps remind them of the delta of the Nile.

All the same, they experienced several distressing years there when, dislodged from their nests, pursued and shot at, it appeared either that they were destined to a rapid end or that the Camargue was condemned to see them vanish for ever from its shores.

Most fortunately the Société d'Acclimatation has put all that to rights, by prohibiting the hunting of the flamingoes. They have therefore returned in full confidence to construct their truncated, conical nests between the two arms of the Rhone.

It even seems as if henceforth the flamingoes will belong to the Camargue for ever. . . .

Like a flower that flies
Over Malagroy and Gines

[4] A wicker racket, slipped over the wrist, to throw and catch the ball in the Basque game of *pellota* (trs).

. . . as Baroncelli sang of them.

Among the birds of prey, marsh harriers and kestrels are familiar sights in the Camargue, while the golden eagle is a very occasional visitor.

Among the smaller but no less interesting species are various types of tern, Kentish plovers, rollers, bee eaters, hoopoes, pratincoles, golden orioles, great reed and other warblers and, for the benefit of the hunter, red-legged partridges.

Finally, night brings the little owl, with its plaintive cry; the eagle owl and the barn owl. The last is known as *beuloli*, or the drinker of oil, for legend has it that it consumes the oil of lamps and lanterns.

Apart from the reserve of Vaccarès, on which the protection of the Camargue fauna primarily depends, the biological station of the Tour du Vallat, directed by Professor Hoffman, daily carries out a remarkable contribution towards the preservation and knowledge of birds. By systematic ringing of all the winged creatures which he captures and afterwards sets free, Professor Hoffman is enabled to follow their traces across the world, and to learn that a particular tern travels each year between Labrador and the Cape Verde Islands, Brazil and Tierra del Fuego, and crosses the Atlantic four times in twelve months; or that he would have to go as far as Western Siberia to find, in the middle of summer, the teal which he ringed on the eve of the previous winter.

In 1956, during that terrible winter, Professor Hoffman saved many a flamingo trapped in the ice. Many others—alas!—could not withstand the sudden lowering of the temperature, and became the easy prey of people who like the flavour of wild flesh and who often came, with knives, to dismember them in the frozen marshes. Thus, between December and January, terrible slaughters took place, from which the species has since fortunately been able to recover.

As far as hunting is concerned, one must above all not exaggerate the destruction that it causes. Admittedly the men of the Camargue are natural hunters, and it is even said that those who are not should be considered as poachers. But one fact stands out: the hunter of the Camargue, before being a hunter, is first and foremost Camarguais. He respects the countryside and its laws because he senses the reason for them, and he knows the geographical limits beyond which such and such a bird is inviolable. Therefore one can say that neither the morning nor evening shoots at ducks passing between their roosting places and their daytime haunts, nor the pursuit by boat of coots on the lakes, nor the hunting of teal, woodcock, partridge or sea birds has ever really endangered the preservation of bird life in the Camargue or the character of the delta as a bird sanctuary.

There is no lack of four-footed game, either.

Certainly, since the middle of the nineteenth century, the wolf has practically disappeared. At that time it used to attack flocks of sheep and it was hunted on horseback, in great beats which generally ended in single combat, the man killing the panting and exhausted beast with a naked blade. In this connection there is a story of the *gardian* Roustanié who, in 1820, pursued a wolf for a whole day, caught up with it at twilight, near an abandoned hovel where the animal had sought shelter, struggled with it, strangled it and finally succumbed to his own wounds, while his exhausted horse died a few miles away.

The beaver (*lou vibre*) is becoming more and more rare, and is now hardly ever seen except on the banks of the Lesser Rhone. Here its presence is betrayed by bits of gnawed wood, with which it constructs its lodge and which it sometimes drops by the wayside, or else by stumps of trees felled by its labours and marked by its teeth.

Myxomatosis has accounted for the rabbits which at one time swarmed on the islets in the large lakes, and the various attempts to re-establish them have so far practically failed.

On the other hand hares and foxes flourish there in numbers and wild boar to a lesser degree. The second, the great enemy of the research station of the Tour du Vallat, whose nets it robs, is difficult to hunt, because of the lack of paths on which it can be shot and of room to follow it with hounds.

As regards the boar, their favourite place remains the Bois des Rièges, where it is strictly prohibited to approach them. But they come out readily for long and often fatal jaunts across the lakes —they are excellent swimmers—the marshes and the *sansouire*.

We should also mention otters, whose fur has a certain value and which frequent the stretches of shallow water and the canals; badgers, which are equally difficult to hunt, polecats, ferrets, weasels and so on.

To complete this picture, certainly incomplete, of the fauna of the Camargue, we must not forget the tortoises and lizards, or the inoffensive grass snakes, the most striking of which is the 'striped snake' with four black lines on a yellow-grey ground, which can attain a length of six feet and the thickness of an arm.

Neither should we overlook the eels of Le Vaccarès, which give rise to what is almost a fishing industry. They are consumed on the spot, in a sort of stew, with a sauce so strong that it is known as 'rust', or sent by van to the Netherlands. There they are smoked and cured before, very often, being returned to France. Thus one can find, in the shops in Arles, Camargue eels, naturalized Dutch, which before being eaten have made the return journey between that country where the water imposes its law on the earth, and that other where the earth has to be won from the water.

Last but not least there are the mosquitoes, for some the plague of the Camargue, for others its surest protection. For the slight tingle of their first attacks, or even the mere menace of their concerted onslaughts, has caused the flight of more than one frail visitor.

However irritating and enterprising they may be, the Camargue mosquitoes are neither tough nor very dangerous. On the one hand, the least puff of wind hinders their flight and prevents them from stinging. On the other hand, specialists are agreed that, in spite of their mode of existence, there is not the least danger of their transmitting malaria.

And then, as so often happens in nature, only the female stings!

It is true that they far outnumber their male companions.

More than once I have paid for watching a lovely sunset over the marshes by having, at dawn the next day, two swollen hands and a pretty well deformed face.

It was, after all, not too dear a price to pay.

7

THE SONS OF THE WIND

WHERE do they come from?

From the land where the sun rises, some of them say.

Could they be descended from the former inhabitants of a mysterious Atlantis, and might they be brothers of the American Indians, whom they often resemble in more than one way?

Baroncelli supported this theory.

Were they already living in Provence before the arrival of the Holy Marys?

Old legends lead us to suppose so. According to these, a gipsy tribe established on the Mediterranean coast, of whom Sarah was one, is said in fact to have welcomed Mary Jacobé and Mary Salomé.

In any case, what is certain is that, nomads by blood and lovers of freedom by vocation, the gipsies were born to enjoy life at the heart of the delta. They have a respect for its traditions, faith in the horse and the bull, a tendency to dream and a certain lyricism, and their music, after all, expresses the Camargue almost as well as do the most authentic Provençal melodies.

Each year then, the sons of the wind meet on May the 24th to celebrate the memory of the saints, and particularly that of Sarah, their patron saint.

More than a week before the start of the pilgrimage their columns stretch along the road that leads from Arles to Les Saintes-Maries. It must be admitted, however, that motor cars of every kind, from the rickety van to the showman's luxurious caravan and the successful horse dealer's Cadillac, are replacing more and more the old horse-drawn caravans of the tinker and the chair mender from Perpignan and the Porte de Montreuil.

But that does not matter, for as soon as they pitch camp in

the square in front of the town hall, round the statue of Mireille[1] and at the foot of the grey cement bull ring, all this vanishes and is recomposed in a perfect harmony of browns, and blood-red and gold lights, intermingled with pungent odours, strange accents and frenzied rhythms.

Each year, moreover, the gipsy encampment encroaches a little more on the village itself. It overflows like boiling milk from the places reserved for it. It stretches across small alleys and between the houses, devouring every inch of free space. It triumphs, it sings, it dances, it snores, it drinks—it is alive.

And thus it is every year.

The same multicoloured and tawdry finery seems to be hanging out to dry between the caravans from one year to the next.

The same smells of spices and aniseed, of sweat, of frying and incense seem to rise from the ground.

Naked children play with the dogs between the horses' hoofs.

The girls go about in groups, their eyes alluring, ready to lance fire.

The men saunter about, dragging a worm-eaten guitar in the dust, stopping anywhere according to their mood and striking a chord which is quickly heard by some adolescent whose face is both brutal and sweet. The latter then draws near, claps his hands and begins to wail and to moan some raucous *flamenco* song.

It was the Bishop of Marseille who, by an order of January 7, 1449, fixed on May 24th (the saint's day of Mary Jacobé) and October 22nd (the saint's day of Mary Salomé) the two annual ceremonies of lowering the shrines containing the remains of the saints and kept in the high chapel of the fortress church. It was thus that the dates for the two pilgrimages, the first of which attracts the larger crowds, were established. Furthermore, the shrines are lowered a third time, on the first Sunday in December, that is, the one nearest to the Feast of the Revelation[2] which is the anniversary of the discovery of the relics.

In reality, the cult of the Holy Marys was in existence in Pro-

[1] Heroine in a dramatic poem of that name by Frédéric Mistral, the Provençal poet; later it was made into an opera by Gounod (trs).
[2] A purely local fête (trs).

vence well before 1449, but from that date onwards it started, little by little, to assume the form that we know today. We should also note the brief interruption brought about by the French Revolution. On March 5, 1794, the church was, in fact, sacked by looters, who laid hands on the reliquaries and set them on fire. But the *curé* of Les Saintes had foreseen what would happen. Helped by one of his parishioners he had, a few days before, taken the precious remains from their chests and then buried them. Three years later they were removed from their hiding place and enclosed in new shrines, similar to the old ones, which are those one can see today.

On the first day of the pilgrimage, that is to say May 24th, at about four in the afternoon, the bells start to ring, calling the faithful to the lowering of the shrines.

The church is soon packed and, as usual, almost in darkness; for, as it was a fortress, the light enters only through narrow windows reminiscent of loopholes.

The people of Provence crowd into the nave and the gallery at the back, and the mass of gipsies into the choir, just by the place where the shrines will be lowered.

The vespers start. Either the *curé*, a priest whom it is desired to honour or, more often, the Archbishop of Aix-en-Provence pronounces the 'Salutation to the Saints'. As soon as his address is finished the crowd intones the *Magnificat*, and the window of the high chapel slowly opens, giving a first sight of the shrines.

What follows is a truly astonishing spectacle.

Held by ropes, the two shrines gradually descend from above the heads of the faithful who, after each verse of the hymn, shout at the tops of their voices and with all the ardour of their Provençal or other accents, 'Long live the Holy Marys! Long live Saint Sarah!'

The hundreds of candles that the pilgrims are carrying are now lit, and make the dark nave scintillate with their slim, golden flames.

And the gipsies, massed in the choir, start to close in, jostling each other and trying to leap up from where they stand in an effort to be the first to touch the holy wood of the shrines.

Women hold up their children at arms' length.

Cripples are hoisted on to their brothers' shoulders, awaiting a miracle.

The cries, the chanting and the acclamations are redoubled.

After the shrines have touched the ground there is a slow but tumultuous procession as far as the sea, to which the gipsies carry the statue of Sarah, with her tiny black head and golden crown emerging from her white satin cloak.

It was in 1935 that, for the first time, the effigy of Sarah was taken out of the crypt where it remains for the rest of the year. The *Nacioun gardiano* then also presented to the gipsies the shield on which they place the statue. They also admitted to their ranks Coucou and Titi (the prince[3]), to show their friendship with the people of the sons of the wind.

Preceded by the *gardians* on horseback, trident in hand, the gipsies and the Provençal crowd then go down towards the sea, amidst a confusion of hymns, prayers, invocations and cries of every kind.

'*Li Boumian sian catouli!*'[4] they chant, almost in chorus. According to strict liturgical convention, this is perhaps not quite correct, but that does not matter at this moment. Moreover, among the people of Les Saintes, Arles and Languedoc who are present, how many are Protestant or free thinkers! Roger Delagnes, socialist mayor of Les Saintes-Maries-de-la-Mer, sings at the top of his voice by the side of the *curé*. And, during these days of pilgrimage, there is a perpetual intermingling of the sacred and the profane, the juxtaposition of a purely Christian religion—that of the Provençal pilgrims—and the faith of the gipsies with its at times confusing manifestations, which very often mix idolatry with prayer.

When the procession at last reaches the beach where boats in vivid colours lie on the pale sand, as if placed there by Van Gogh, the *gardians* ride into the water up to their horses' flanks, and many of the gipsies go in up to their waists. The spray whips Sarah's face and cloak. Who would then dream of bothering

[3] In fact, there is neither a prince nor a king of the gipsies, but only certain men who, owing to their age and experience, wield authority over several families or tribes.
[4] 'The gipsies are Catholics!'

about such questions as to whether the servant of the saints came from Provence, Egypt, Palestine or Atlantis?

It is ten o'clock in the evening.

On the terrace of an open-air café, facing the sea, the gipsies have formed a large circle, and the first festivities of the pilgrimage begin.

I have passed entire nights at Les Saintes, mixing with the gipsies without ever being mistaken for one of them, but also without ever making me feel that I was, at bottom, only a *pantrillon* or a *gadgi*, that is to say a stranger to the race of the sons of the wind. I have wandered about among the gipsies, I have been submerged in the tepid and slightly rancid haze that rises from their camps. I have listened to them playing and singing. I have watched them sharply smacking the strings of their guitars with the backs of their hands, or, on the contrary, lovingly caressing them with their finger tips, with the gestures of a harpist. I have contemplated them in their dances, raking the dusty ground with their feet and crisply snapping their twinkling brown fingers, their whole bodies swaying and cracking like whips.

One evening, in a café where the gipsies were drinking and where I was alone at a table with a glass of aniseed before me, a small girl about twelve years old came and placed her hand on my shoulder, stretching out the other hand to beg for money. She had a minute face, in which, in spite of the dust, I could see her eyes—two sad eyes, weary with late nights and so large that they seemed to reach back indefinitely and almost disappear under the black waves of her hair.

She looked at me in silence, gravely, her hand held out with no hint of humility in a most natural manner. I said to her: 'Sing me something first, and then I will give you 100 francs!' With a nod of the head she accepted my offer, then, without my being able to foresee her gesture, she grasped the glass in front of me and emptied it in one gulp. She staggered slightly, her eyes wavering, and I noticed that they were already gorged with alcohol, as was her entire body. She half opened her mouth to sing, and collapsed gently, without however breaking the glass of which she had not let go. From a nearby table three youths

57

got up slowly—her brothers, or perhaps her cousins. I helped them to pick up the child and they carried her away into the night, without speaking a word but just giving me a smile of excuse.

I left the café in my turn and crossed the village, all illuminated, and the fair with its roundabouts, its shooting galleries, its nougat stalls and its fortune tellers. Then I drew near the church, whose crenellated battlements pierced the obscurity.

I knew that the gipsies who were not dancing or singing in the cafés, in the streets, in the squares or between the caravans would be spending the night in the damp crypt, crowded round the statue of the Black Virgin of the Bohemians. I also knew that I should be forbidden to go down there, and that I would only be able to hear the songs from afar off, as in a shadow play—the negative image, as it were, of these prayers, these murmurs, these wailings so like *flamenco* songs. I could only imagine the haloes round the candles, floating above the sanctuary and slowly rising up the steps that lead to the crypt, swallowing up little by little the darkness of the nave and the choir. I would perhaps smell the fumes of incense, mixed with the reek of alcohol rising from the gipsies at prayer. But the stones and the night would guard intact for the nomad race the mysteries of their cult.

All this in fact happened, and yet I regretted none of the hours that I spent in the church, trying to divine from its echoes the inaccessible vigil of the gipsies, hidden in the bowels of the earth.

It is on the second day of the pilgrimage, after the vespers of the afternoon, that the faithful are again to be found in the church, and that the shrines are raised with the same ceremonial and perhaps with even more fervour than before.

At times, when the shrines begin to rise, women and children hang on to them and are lifted from the ground. The procedure must then be interrupted and the precious coffers lowered again, and only when their superfluous load has been removed can they once more start to ascend.

After the religious ceremonies are over, bull and *gardian* contests take place in the arena: branding, competitions between animals from different herds, displays of horsemanship and so on.

And, as soon as night falls, music and dancing again take possession of the village.

All over the camps, and all along the beach, fingers snap, hands clap and guitars accompany anew the wails of *flamenco* singing.

Certain smoky cafés off the road that leads to the Lesser Rhone are the meeting places of *tzigane* violinists, whose strings invoke the nostalgia of the great steppes and the frenzied spirit of the *czardas*.

Over there it is Andalusia; here it is central Europe.

Violins, guitars, laments and love songs will now continue until the first flush of dawn above the marshes.

Then, one by one, cars, motor and horse-drawn caravans and the light carts of the sons of the wind again take to the road, leaving the *sansouire* and the lakes, the herds and the flights of flamingoes, for that country with no frontiers which from day to day is recreated by their mood and their blood.

But on the next May 24th they will be there. For all gipsy roads lead to Les Saintes-Maries.

8

LAND OF COCKAIGNE

A CAMARGUE friend said to me one day : 'In the Camargue there is
first of all the Rhone and then the sun. The first fertilizes the soil,
on condition that one takes a little trouble to cultivate it. The
second makes men content with their lot. At Les Saintes-Maries,
for example, everybody more or less owns something, whether
it be his hut, his vines or his boat. The man from Les Saintes has
two pair of slippers in summer, and one pair of *sabots* in winter,
and with that he is content. He fishes, hunts, plants, hoes, plays
the mason and builds castles in the air. . . .'

'Builds castles in the air?'

'Yes, he dreams, you see. He imagines a thousand and one
adventures or pleasures, and he gets more out of them in this
way than if they actually happened to him one day. In fact he
would not exchange his universe for anything in the world.
Nobody worries about things. At Les-Saintes-Maries any small
business pays if it is well run. There is the blue sky and the sun,
and there are many more fish than one could, or would want to,
catch, and there is never a single death at sea because the saints
protect the fisherman. Here one lives as in the Bible. The Land of
Cockaigne, that's what it is!'

To appreciate this happy knack of day dreaming, this freedom
from worrying about life, both of which are among the traits of
the Camargue character, you need only go about midday to Boisset's, the big café situated opposite the town hall of Les Saintes.
Here you will most certainly be far removed from the infinite
silence and solitude of the *sansouire* or the marshes, but the
Camargue is there, none the less.

At the counter, behind which Boisset himself supervises with
authority and good humour the amount of *pastis* consumed,
everyone lets himself go, swaps yarns, boasts a bit and jokes,

whether he be a *gardian*, a fisherman, a poacher or a keeper.

You would often think that you were listening to characters from Daudet.

François Périer, the head *gardian* of Cacharel, is one of the stars of the place, by reason of his talent as a horseman as well as by the resemblance of his name to that of the actor who created the part of Bobosse in the film with that title. He is discussing the breaking of horses with Guy. The latter hires out horses at Le Pont des Banes, and some of the more snobbish lady visitors willingly take him for a Provençal nobleman, because he is known quite simply by the name of Guy du Pont des Banes.

At one table Jacques Pioch, the rice grower, is playing a game of cards worthy of Marcel Pagnol with Roger Delagnes, the mayor of the biggest *commune*[1] in France in area (about eighty-nine acres). With them are Doctor Cambon, with his mane of white silk, who is the least busy man of Les Saintes where the salt air is good for the health, and Yvan Audouard, poet by birth, prose writer by profession, lover of the bull ring by vocation and Camargue horseman by force of circumstance.

Zézé, nicknamed 'la Boumian' because the inn that he keeps bears that name, and Roger Fages, called 'le Caballero' because he was the pupil of the famous bullfighter Charles Fidani, enter next. They are followed by Barbut, bending his legs till they almost form a perfect circle, while his forage cart, harnessed with a pure Camargue horse, waits in front of the covered terrace for Yves Brayer to transfer it on to a sheet of white paper in ten strokes of his charcoal pencil.

At the end of the room 'lou prince' holds his debonair court. He is not the head of a gipsy tribe, raised to noble rank by popular favour, but an authentic Belgian prince of royal blood, Beaudoin de Lignes, who preferred the Midi to the north, and the Camargue of his dreams to life in a castle.

That the prince appreciates good cheer is proved by his girth and his appearance. That he loves *pastis* morning, noon and night, and whenever his throat becomes dry, is clearly apparent from the rhythm and conviction with which he consumes this sunny drink. One does not need to hold a lengthy conversation with him to realize that he relishes broad stories. But that

[1] An administrative parish (trs).

he is a 'good prince', in the most democratic and most Camargue sense of the term, is agreed upon to such an extent by all the inhabitants of Les Saintes, Beauduc, Albaron and other places that if he decided one day to add to his titles of nobility the names of a good dozen localities in the Camargue, the municipal councils would fall over themselves to obtain the favour of his choice.

Les Saintes-Maries-de-la-Mer thus numbers several characters who may be surprising to the uninitiated, but who, in the same way as a colony of celebrities would do, have become inseparable from the little world of the Camargue.

For instance, I have only to think of Laurent Roche, called 'le Shérif' because, during the heroic days of the silent cinema, he invariably played the role of sheriff in the films that were made by Joé Hamman near Le Sauvage and Clamador. Today the sheriff, with his broad-brimmed, black felt hat crammed down on his white hair, and his brick-red face, continues to show off his well-built figure in front of any ciné cameras that happen to be there, and to play a somewhat plump Buffalo Bill before the young Swedish, Bavarian and even Parisian ladies who come to hire from him reasonably docile horses in order to venture into that Camargue which is so exciting in their imagination.

For a long time there was also Clanclan, an old native of Les Saintes, with a white, fan-shaped beard, who was keeper of the *toril*[2] on the days of the contests, a great hunter, municipal crossing sweeper, brander, castrator, grave digger and chief dreamer. At times you would meet him on certain moonlight nights, on the breakwater by the sea, riding a bicycle from another age. By tradition you had to call out to him:

'*Hou! Clanclan, mounte vas?*'

'*Voy à mi casteu.*'[3]

I could also mention Dona Preciosa, a resident gipsy who knows how much of their future she should tell the inhabitants of Les Saintes so as to encourage them to remain what they are. Then there is the Belgian Anne-Marie, who hires out horses, or again Baraque, who fishes for small shellfish known as *tellines*.

---

[2] Pen where the bulls are kept; see p. 28 (trs).

[3] 'Oh, Clanclan! Where are you going?'
  'I'm going to my castles.'

He had romanced so much about a fabulous inheritance which had been left to him by distant Spanish cousins that one fine day he was taken at his word: certain journalists chartered an aeroplane to fly him to the coast of Alicante to recover his wealth and put an end to his dreams.

But I must reserve a special place in this gallery for Sarah Astruc, whose small white house, standing near the edge of the village, bears the sign of the bull. Sarah is the veritable guardian angel of Les Saintes, the good fairy, the friend, the refuge of all the wrecks, the poets and the dreamers of the delta. She says that she is not a gipsy by race and that she owes her Christian name only to the sympathetic generosity of her friends, the sons of the wind. But the latter do not make mistakes. If they have accorded Sarah the name of their patron saint, they have very good reasons for doing so. Although Sarah may not be a gipsy by birth, she is one in effect at heart and by vocation. And on the nights when the moon is full she herself is closer to Mithras than all her would-be relatives are, at that moment, to her.

In various ways all these characters are part of the scenery of Les Saintes-Maries-de-la-Mer. They are of the Camargue in the purest sense and so entirely part of it that, on the day that a maker of *santons*[4] should come to seek inspiration in the village of the two Marys and Sarah, it is they who will be seen in a circle round Jesus, who will be lying on a bed of *salicornia*, between a horse from Cacharel and a bull from Le Grand Radeau.

[4] Small painted clay figures used in Provençal Christmas cribs (trs).

9

SANCTUARY OF SPACE AND THE WIND

NEARLY 450 miles from Paris by road, and less than 50 miles from Marseille as the crow flies, the Camargue is one of the last natural wonders of our time, demanding more of its own people than of technique or science.

Galloping at sunset behind fifty or so bulls and cows from L'Amarée, how many times has it not dawned on me that an hour later I should be at Arles, that from there, during the same evening, I should take a train smelling of the dusty night, and that the next morning, in Paris, I should find myself in a studio in the rue Cognacq-Jay, under the projectors and behind the television cameras. Quite frankly, this made me lose all notions of space and time. . . .

A traveller by air, whose eyes were bandaged during a fifteen-hour flight from Orly, which landed him finally—supposing that one could land there—at one of the points of the Etang de la Grande-Gorgue or towards the Gaze des Deux Lionnes, would find it very difficult to point out on a map of the world the approximate position of where he thought he was. The delta of the Nile, the infinite solitude of the Canadian Great Lakes, the dreary spaces of South Dakota, or, if he caught sight of the edges of the Bois des Rièges, the scrubby banks of the Ogowe River. His wandering imagination could roam at will until he had at last been given the key to the problem: a triangle of salt, sand and water, with its angles pointing to the vineyards of Hérault, the Roman arena at Arles and the modern petrol port of Lavéra.

Because it is at once miracle and mirage, and in order that it may remain for as long as possible what the wind, the sun and the dreams of its admirers have made it, the Camargue merits all our vigilance and all our care.

In fact, dangers are lying in wait for the region and, so as to get a grip on it, they often outwardly bear the most innocuous and reassuring aspects.

Just after the second world war, for instance, the Camargue of the *gardians* saw the arrival of a redoubtable enemy which, under the honourable pretext of satisfying French appetites, ran the risk of subduing the countryside to its own voracity—rice. In the north of the delta, and along the branches of the Rhone, immense surfaces were ploughed up, irrigated and made to produce such huge quantities of such delicious rice that many farmers began to look with interest on the marshy lands which, up till then, they had despised. The warning was sharp, and the danger has not yet completely disappeared. Nowadays, nearly 77 square miles of rice fields produce each year 80,000 tons of rice, which is three-quarters of France's annual consumption. It goes without saying that all the land belonging to cultivators of rice is henceforth forbidden territory to the bulls and horses. Besides this, the waste water, full of hormones, which runs off the rice fields, kills the saline vegetation and the fish in the lakes.

Nevertheless, the danger signal has been given and the rice combines seem to be content with their actual boundaries. Let us hope so, but let us also be on guard, for economics, under the most honourable pretexts in the world, can soon stifle poetry, and that which is prematurely called the development of a region can kill other rare and precious qualities in it. All the same, it is a well-established fact that the rice grower, even if he was not born in the delta of the Rhone, becomes an adopted son of the Camargue very much quicker than the true Camargue—that of the *sansouire*, the marshes and the herds of bulls—turns into rice fields. On the whole this is reassuring.

Today, however, another and more sinister danger threatens the Camargue: tourism. Admittedly it brings in dollars, marks and other hard currencies, that is to say, wealth. But, against that, it means installing electricity and running water so that enthusiasts can lead a rough life in the so-called *gardians'* bungalows which building contractors are running up by mass-production methods on the outskirts of Les Saintes-Maries. On the other hand, if *homo touristicus* is intent in coming to the Camargue to find solitude there, he is wrong in only one thing, and that is to

E

look for it in a crowd. The few resigned hacks hired out to him by jobbing stables, whose corrals also continue to increase in the neighbourhood of Les Saintes, are there to help him in his search. The flamboyant shirts, the trousers fitting too tightly and the wide-brimmed hats, which he can buy in special shops in the village, do the rest.

It is also true that the tourist is sometimes more demanding. He is astonished that the bulls do not wait for him, two deep, all along both sides of the road from Arles. He asks where he can visit the gipsy 'reserves' and deplores the fact that the flamingoes are not in cages, like canaries. Fortunately the Camargue has a sense of humour!

It was Denys Colomb de Daunant, *manadier*, poet and film maker, who founded the first club where visitors could find a bed, food and a horse, by the side of the lake at Cacharel, and thus might try to discover the Camargue. But Denys Colomb is so fond of, and so sensitive to, the world of the Camargue that he thought he was serving it in helping to reveal it in this way. To those who had admired the scenery in his films it gave the chance of catching a glimpse of the real thing. The idea was a tempting one.

Success, however, is always contagious, and the example was widely followed. For better or for worse. That is why certain inhabitants of the Camargue nowadays reproach Denys Colomb de Daunant of having played the sorcerer's apprentice.

One day I myself reproached him about this, to find out what he would say in his own defence.

'As it is inconceivable in the twentieth century to keep quiet about or to hide the Camargue,' he said to me, 'and as it would be the height of egoism on our part to keep it from our fellow creatures, I think it is better that it should be revealed with our consent than without it. Besides, even if twenty thousand tourists invaded Les Saintes-Maries, we should only have to go a mile to regain the wilds and peace, and there would be very few people who would follow us.'

This reply seemed to me to be both wise and convincing.

The Camargue has, moreover, excellent means of natural defence to enable it to remain the great sanctuary of the wind, of space and secrecy, of legends and silence, of wisdom and adventure, that we wish it to be. It has existed for centuries, inundating Roman towns, swallowing up legions and herds of bulls. All the works of man within it are but written in sand, and are therefore predestined to vanish one day.

Cabanes de Gines, Les Saintes-Maries-de-la-Mer,
and Paris, 1960

67

GLOSSARY OF LOCAL TERMS

abrivado: the ceremony of conducting the bulls for a cocarde contest from the corral to the bull ring.

anouble: a yearling bull calf.

bayle-gardian: head gardian, farm bailiff.

beuoli: barn owl.

biou, lou: the bull; *li biou*: the bulls.

bouvino: lovers or amateurs of bull fights.

chivau: horse.

cocarde: the rosette placed on a bull's forehead for a contest; the contest in which the rosette is removed.

corrida: Spanish type of bull fight, or *mise à mort*, in which the bull is put to death.

Coupo Santo: the meridional anthem.

débrandage: the ceremony of breaking in horses; rodeo.

devise: the colours of a *manade* or herd of bulls.

doublen: a two-year-old bull calf.

embarcador: a passage from which the bulls are 'embarked' on a lorry for a contest.

engano: the Provençal name for salicornia or marsh samphire.

escapada: the escape of a bull from the *abrivado*.

escoussuro: a nick or cut in a bull's ear, to show to which *manade* he belongs.

estocade: the death blow in a *mise à mort* bull fight

étang: a lake.

félibre: a member of a society of Provençal poets and scholars founded by Frédéric Mistral (1830-1914).

ferrade: the ceremony of branding bulls.

gardian: a man who looks after herds of horses and bulls.

gardianou: an apprentice *gardian*.

gaze: a stretch of not very deep water.

grasiho: the sizzling noise, the actual branding of a bull.

manade: a herd of bulls and cows; estate where these are reared.

manadier: owner of herds of bulls, rancher and stock-breeder.

mas:	a Provençal country house; farm.
Midi:	the south of France.
mourraioun:	a rope bridle.
mourrau, museu:	a half-moon shaped willow stick used to muzzle yearling bull calves.
mourven:	Phoenician juniper.
muselado:	the ceremony of muzzling or weaning a yearling bull calf.
Nacioun gardiano:	a society of *gardians*, founded by the Marquis de Baroncelli.
pastis:	an alcoholic aniseed drink.
querencia:	a place in the arena where the bull seeks refuge.
quite:	the action of trying to attract the bull's attention, to draw it away from something he is attacking, in a *mise à mort* bull fight.
radeau:	a sand bank or small island of sand.
raseteur, razeteur:	a man who, in a cocarde contest, tries to snatch the rosette from the bull and in doing so brushes so close by the animal that he almost grazes or shaves by him.
roubine:	a narrow irrigation canal.
saladelle:	statice or sea lavender.
salicornia:	marsh samphire or glasswort.
sansouire:	a stretch of alluvial soil, covered with saline vegetation.
santons:	small painted plaster figures used in Provençal Christmas cribs.
seden:	a horsehair lasso.
segonnal—aux:	stretches of land between the banks and the embankments of the two Rhones.
simbeu:	the leading bull of a herd, with a bell round his neck.
toril:	an enclosure, or pen, inside the bull ring, where the bulls are kept before they enter the arena.
trident:	a three-pronged iron fork, in the shape of a crescent moon, mounted on a long wooden handle, and used by gardians to control bulls and horses.
vedel:	calf.
vibre, lou:	beaver.

Herds (*manades*) of bulls from Provence and Languedoc:
ear notches, branding marks and colours
Diagram by Gérard Gadiot

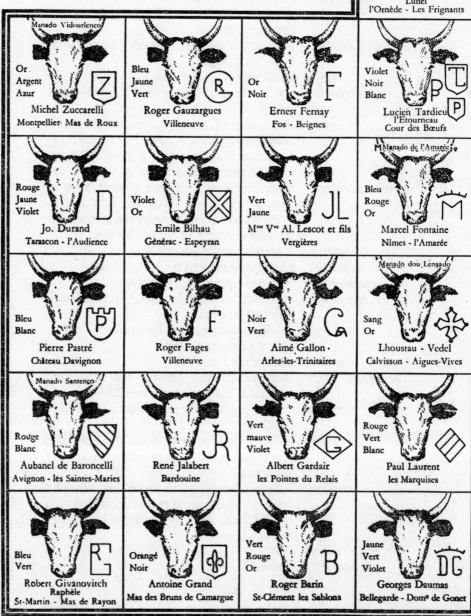

Rouge
Noir

Mme Vve Jean Rebuffat et fils
Lunel
l'Ornède - Les Frignants

Manado Vidourlenco

Or
Argent
Azur

Michel Zuccarelli
Montpellier· Mas de Roux

Bleu
Jaune
Vert

Roger Gauzargues
Villeneuve

Or
Noir

Ernest Fernay
Fos - Beignes

Violet
Noir
Blanc

Lucien Tardieu
l'Etourneau
Cour des Bœufs

Rouge
Jaune
Violet

Jo. Durand
Tarascon - l'Audience

Violet
Or

Emile Bilhau
Générac - Espeyran

Vert
Jaune

Mme Vve Al. Lescot et fils
Vergières

Bleu
Rouge
Or

Marcel Fontaine
Nimes - l'Amarée

Manado de l'Amarée

Bleu
Blanc

Pierre Pastré
Château Davignon

Roger Fages
Villeneuve

Noir
Vert

Aimé Gallon·
Arles-les-Trinitaires

Sang
Or

Lhoustau - Vedel
Calvisson - Aigues-Vives

Manado dou Lenaado

Rouge
Blanc

Aubanel de Baroncelli
Avignon - les Saintes-Maries

René Jalabert
Bardouine

Vert
mauve
Violet

Albert Gardair
les Pointes du Relais

Rouge
Vert
Blanc

Paul Laurent
les Marquises

Manado Santenço

Bleu
Vert

Robert Givanovitch
Raphèle
St-Martin - Mas de Rayon

Orangé
Noir

Antoine Grand
Mas des Bruns de Camargue

Vert
Rouge
Or

Roger Barin
St-Clément les Sablons

Jaune
Vert
Violet

Georges Daumas
Bellegarde - Dome de Gonet

70

François André
...es - Capeau - la Fourbine

Bleu
Rouge
Jaune
Marius Tardieu
Albert Espelly
Tour du Vallat

Bleu
Jaune
Henri Mathieu
Codognan
l'Audience - Dions

Azur
Or
Mᵉˡˡᵉ Guillerme
Seignoret

Jaune
Rouge
Joseph Sol
Basses-Méjanes

Raoux
Lansac

Gris clair
Blanc
Denys Colomb de Daunant
Cacharel

Vert
Blanc
Hubert Yonnet
la Bélugo

Tricolore
Etienne Saurel
Fos-sur-Mer

Violet
Rouge
Or
Fernand Gidde
l'Eyssclle

Fernand Féraud
Saintes-Maries - Capeau

Soc. Nat. d'Acclimatation

Pierre Carrut
Fos-sur-Mer - la Fossette

Vert
Blanc
Bleu
Fabre - Mailhan
Cabanes de Romieu
les Bernacles

Jaune
Bleu ciel
André Pourquier
Amphise

Pierre Saurel
Fos-sur-Mer - la Sonde

Blanc
Noir
Tricolore
Nou de la Houplière
Arles

Vert
Jaune
Orange
Frédéric Clément
Codognan - Raphèle

Vert
Orangé
Arthur et Alfred Blatière
Vergèze - le Courréjau

les
Couleurs
de l'
Arc-en-Ciel
le Petit-Badon

arcel et Jean Raynaud
Le Sauvage

Jaune
Violet
Noir
Louis Thiers
Méjanes

Blanc
Noir
Rose
Jean Thibaud
Saliers

Rouge
Vert
Jean Laffont
Ste-Anne

Vert
Jaune
Rouge
Paul Autheman
les Saintes-Maries

Jacques Raynaud
Sylveréal - le Sauvage

Rouge
Violet
Auguste Bertet
le Cavaou

Gris
Noir
Jean Cambi
Beaucaire - Cabassole

Bleu
Jaune
Rouge
Paul Ricard
Méjanes

Vert
Noir
Rouge
André Deville
Georges Ribaud
Arles - Mollèges

G. Gadiot • Arles • 1961

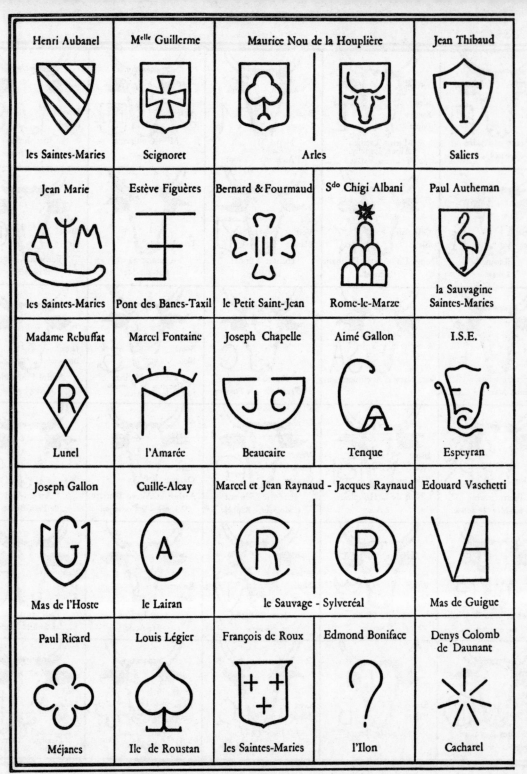

Henri Aubanel	Mᵉˡˡᵉ Guillerme	Maurice Nou de la Houplière		Jean Thibaud
les Saintes-Maries	Seignoret	Arles		Saliers
Jean Marie	Estève Figuères	Bernard & Fourmaud	Sᵈᵒ Chigi Albani	Paul Autheman
les Saintes-Maries	Pont des Bancs-Taxil	le Petit Saint-Jean	Rome-le-Marze	la Sauvagine Saintes-Maries
Madame Rebuffat	Marcel Fontaine	Joseph Chapelle	Aimé Gallon	I.S.E.
Lunel	l'Amarée	Beaucaire	Tenque	Espeyran
Joseph Gallon	Cuillé-Alcay	Marcel et Jean Raynaud - Jacques Raynaud		Edouard Vaschetti
Mas de l'Hoste	le Lairan	le Sauvage - Sylveréal		Mas de Guigue
Paul Ricard	Louis Légier	François de Roux	Edmond Boniface	Denys Colomb de Daunant
Méjanes	Ile de Roustan	les Saintes-Maries	l'Ilon	Cacharel

G. Gadiot   Arles. 1962

Branding marks of Camargue horses
Diagram by Gérard Gadiot

72

Emile Bilhau	Antoine Grand	André Merville	Marcel Mailhan	Guy Lapeyre
Espeyran	Mas des Bruns de Camargue	les Arcis Vouzon Sologne	Gimeaux	Mas Neuf du Vaccarès
Colcombet-Etienne	Lhoustau & Vedel Manado dóu Lengado	Louis Lacroix	Fabre & Mailhan	de Garam
Mas du Roure	Calvisson	les Enfores de l'Eysselle	Cabanes de Romieu	les Trinitaires
Roger Gauzargues	Roland Fraissinet	Soc. Civile Agricole du Domaine de	Albert Espelly	Gourdon
Antonelle	le Lairan	la Vernède	les Saintes-Maries	Vauvert
Bernard Daydé Manado de la Mar		Cte Agr. de la Crau	Vives-Apy	Robert Givanovitch
Valagus - le Lairan		Mas Thibert le Retour des Aires	Mas d'Icard de Crau	Raphèle Mas de Rayon
Henri Dupuis	Clarac & Clauzel	Auguste Puig	Poulain d'Andecy	Charles Mignard
Giraud	les Grandes Cabanes du Valcarès	Aigues-Mortes	Aigues-Mortes	Arles

ILLUSTRATIONS

74

25 and 26: Branding horses, carried out by Denys Colomb de Daunant at the Mas de Cacharel.

27: Branding iron for bulls (Manade Aubanel).

28: Jacques Raynaud.

29: Cocarde bulls in a lorry on the way to a contest.

30 and 31: *Abrivado* at Vauvert.

32: Two bulls escape at Saint-Laurent-d'Aigouze.

33: Leaving the bull ring (*bandide*) at Les Saintes-Maries-de-la-Mer.

34: Contest at Aigues-Mortes.

35: A *razeteur's* hook or *razet*.

36 and 37: Amateurs in contests with cows.

38: The bull, pursuing the *razeteur*, jumps over the barrier.

39: Only the contestant jumps.

40: Amateur cocarde contest at Marsillargues.

41: Arrival of the *gardians* at the walls of Aigues-Mortes.

42: The tomb of the bull Le Sanglier, at Le Cailar.

43: Typical profile of a Camargue horse.

44: Mares rushing into the corral.

45, 46, 47 and 48: Stallions fighting at Cosan's.

49, 50 and 51: Capturing horses for branding at the Mas de Cacharel.

52: René Barbut.

53: Mane and tail: the nobility of the Camargue horse.

54 and 55: The forehead wide and flat, the nostrils very open.

56: Equestrian feats by *gardians* (he has just snatched the orange off the plate).

57: Phoenician juniper (*mourven*) in the Bois des Rièges.

58: Purple heron.

59: Black kite.

60: Black stork (rare).

61: Herring gull.

62: Duck's eggs.

63: Avocet's eggs.

64: Shells of egret's eggs after hatching.

65: Gull's eggs.

66, 67 and 68: Egrets in flight.

69: Avocet in flight.

70: Tufted duck.

71 and 72: Flamingoes taking wing and in flight.

73: Nightjar.

74: A young egret which has fallen from the nest.

ACKNOWLEDGEMENTS

The photographs numbered 1-7, 9, 13-16, 18, 19, 21-24, 27-39, 40-42, 44-48, 49-52, 54-70, 73-79, 81-89, 90-102, 103-109, 111-116 were taken by Michèle Brabo.

The photographs numbered 8, 10, 11, 12, 17, 25, 26, 43, 53, 80, 110 and the colour photographs numbered I-V were taken by Serge Holtz.

The photographs numbered 71, 72 are the property of Films Montsouris (Paris).

The photograph number 20 is the property of Editions Arthaud, Paris.

LA CAMARGUE

LA CAM

1 et 2. Marais, taureaux, espace.
3. Les taureaux du mas de l'Amarée.
4. La sansouire au petit matin.

ARGUE

PAR MICHEL - DROIT
COUVERTURE D'YVES BRAYER

PHOTOGRAPHIES

DE

MICHÈLE BRABO

ET

SERGE HOLTZ

ARTHAUD

3

6

16. Michel Droit avec les taureaux du mas de l'Amarée.

16

17. Anouble tétant.

17

18. Marcel Raynaud.

19. Gardians au mas de Cacharel.

20

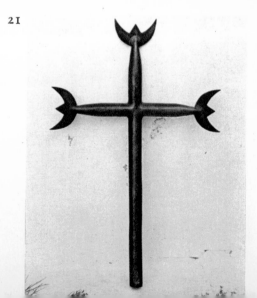

21

20. *Le Marquis Folco de Baroncelli-Javon.*

21. *Croix pour le tombeau du Marquis.*

22. *Au centre, Alphonse Arnaud, capitaine de la* Nacioun Gardiano.

23. *La selle du Marquis de Baroncelli, au musée du Roure, en Avignon.*

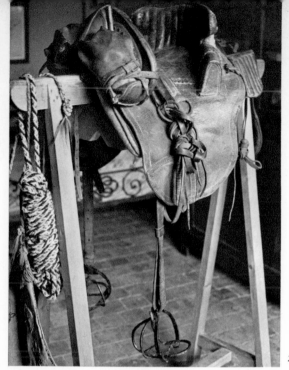

23

24. Taureaux dans le « bouvau »,
au mas du Grand Radeau.

22

25

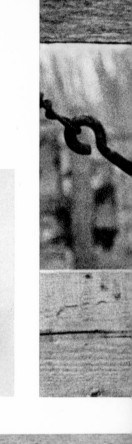

27

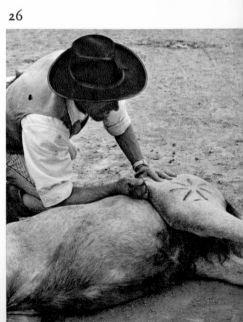

26

25 et 26. Marquage de chevaux exécuté par Denys Colomb de Daunant au mas de Cacharel.

27. Fer pour taureaux (manade Aubanel).

28. Jacques Raynaud.

29. Taureaux « cocardiers » dans le char qui les emmène sur les lieux de la course.

30 et 31. Abrivado à Vauvert.

32. *A Saint-Laurent-d'Aigouze, deux taureaux se sont échappés.*

33. *Sortie des arènes (bandide) aux Saintes-Maries-de-la-Mer.*

34. *Courses à Aigues-Mortes.*

33

34

36

35

35. *Crochet de razeteur (razet).*

36 *et* 37. *Amateurs s'essayant devant des vaches.*

38. *Le taureau, poursuivant le razeteur, a sauté la barrière.*

39. *L'homme est seul à sauter.*

40. *Course libre à Marsillargues.*

41. *Arrivée de gardians le long des remparts d'Aigues-Mortes.*

38

39

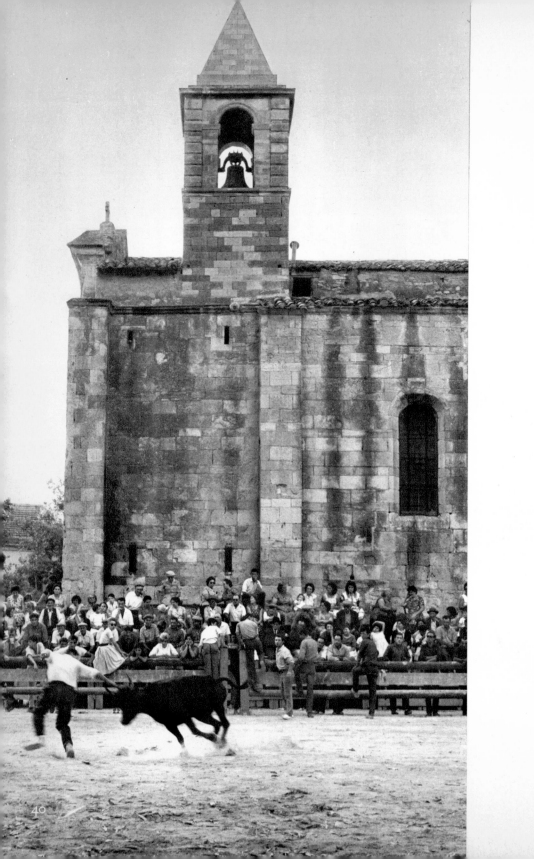

45

46

47

48

45-46-47-48. *Combat d'étalons chez Cosan.*

49

49-50-51. Capture de chevaux pour le marquage, au mas de Cacharel.

52. René Barbut.

53. Crinière et queue: noblesse du cheval de Camargue.

54-55. Front large et plat, naseaux très ouverts.

58. *Héron pourpré.*

59. *Milan royal.*

60. *Cigogne noire (rare).*

61. *Goéland argenté.*

63

64

62. *Œufs de cane.*

63. *Œufs d'avocette.*

64. *Œufs d'aigrette*
    après l'éclosion.

65. *Œufs de goéland.*

66

67

68

69

66, 67, 68. Vol d'aigrettes.

69. Avocette.

70. Canard murillon.

71 et 72. Envol de flamants.

73. Engoulevent.

74. Loriot.

75. Jeune aigrette tombée du nid.

76. Jeune balbuzard (rare).

77. Petits faucons-cresserelles.

73

74

75

78. *Chasse dans les marais.*

79 et 80. Flamants roses.

81. Yves Brayer.

82. Elevage de sangliers chez Fraissinet, au Lairan.

79

80

81

83

83. *Pêche dans le canal du Rhône, entre Aigues-Mortes et Le Grau-du-Roi.*

84 et 85. *Pêche dans les roubines.*

84

85

86

87

86-87-88. La culture du riz.

93

94

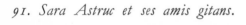

91. *Sara Astruc et ses amis gitans.*

92. *Dans une rue des Saintes-Maries-de-la-Mer.*

93-94-95. *Visages de Fils du Vent.*

95

96. *Dona Preciosa, la voyante gitane des Saintes.*

97. *Un coin du campement des gitans, le long de la mer.*

100

98. *Vénération des châsses.*

99. *Descente des châsses.*

100. *Statue de Sainte Sarah.*

101. *Les statues des Saintes Maries conduites à la mer par les gardians.*

105. René Barbut et Madame Barbut.

106. Arlésiennes.

107. Angèle Vernet, reine d'Arles.

108. *Yves Brayer.*

109. *Jour de fête en Arles sur le boulevard des Lices*

110. Intérieur camarguais.

111. Mas Laffont.

112. Halte dans le Bois des Rièges.

115

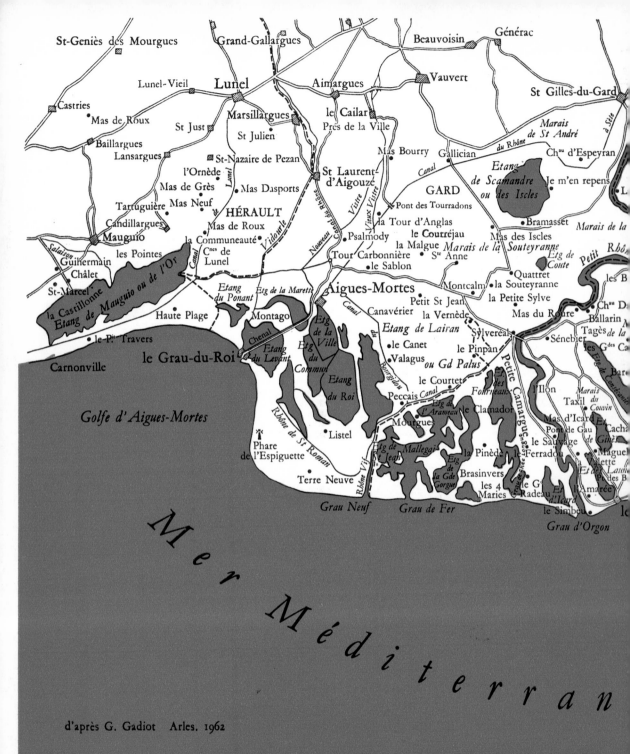

St-Geniès des Mourgues   Grand-Gallargues   Beauvoisin   Générac

Lunel-Vieil   **Lunel**   Aimargues   Vauvert

Castries   St Gilles-du-Gard

Mas de Roux   St Just   Marsillargues   le Cailar   *Marais*
de St André

Baillargues   St Julien   Près de la Ville   Ch²ᵘ d'Espeyran

Lansargues   St-Nazaire de Pezan   Mas Bourry   Gallician   *du Rhône*

l'Ornède   St Laurent-   *Étang*   Je m'en repens
Mas de Grès   d'Aigouzé   *de Scamandre*
ou des Iscles

Tartuguière   Mas Neuf   **GARD**

Candillargues   **HÉRAULT**   Pont des Tourradons   Bramasset   *Marais de la*

Mauguio   Mas de Roux   la Tour d'Anglas   Mas des Iscles
la Communauté   Psalmody   le **Courréjau**   *Étg de*
les Pointes   Cⁿᵉˢ de   la Malgue   *Marais de la* **Souteyranne**   *Coute*

Guihermain   Lunel   Tour Carbonnière   Stᵉ Anne   Quattret   *Petit Rhône*
Châlet   le Sablon   la Souteyranne   les B

St-Marcel   *Étang*   **Aigues-Mortes**   Montcalm   la Petite Sylve   Ch²ᵘ D
la Castillonne   *du Ponant*   *Étg de la Marette*   Petit St Jean   Mas du Roure   Ballarin
Étang de Mauguio ou de l'Or   Canavérion   la Vernède   Tagès *de la*

Haute Plage   Montago   *Étg*   Sylveréal   Sénebier   G⁰ᵉˢ de Ca
de la   *Étang de Lairan*   *Étg Étg de Ca*

le Pᵗ Travers   *Chenal*   *Ville*   le Canet   le Pinpan   *Bare*

Carnonville   **le Grau-du-Roi**   *Étang*   *Étang*   Valagus   *ou Gd Palus*   l'Ilon   *Marais du*
du Levant   *du*   le Courtet   Taxil   *Couvin*
Commun   Peccais   *Étg des*   Mas d'Icard *Et*

Étang   *Canal*   *Fourneaux*   Pont de Gau   Cacha
du Roi   *Étg de*   le Clamador   *de Giu*
Moutgues   *l'Arameau*   le Sauvage   Maguel

Golfe d'Aigues-Mortes   Listel   *Étg de Mallegal*   la Pinède   le Ferradou   *la Valette*
Étg de St Jean   *Et des Laun*
Phare   *Rhône de St Roman*   *Étg*   Brasinvers   *Ptᵉ des B*
de l'Espiguette   *de*   les 4   le G²
Rhône Vif   *la Gde*   Maries   Radeau   *EA*
Terre Neuve   *Gorgue*   *d'Icard*
le Simbeu

Grau Neuf   Grau de Fer   Grau d'Orgon

Mer Méditerran

d'après G. Gadiot   Arles. 1962